US SUPREME COURT LANDMARK CASES

MARRIAGE EQUALITY

Obergefell v. Hodges

JASON PORTERFIELD

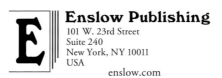

Enslow Publishing
101 W. 23rd Street
Suite 240
New York, NY 10011
USA
enslow.com

Published in 2017 by Enslow Publishing, LLC.
101 W. 23rd Street, Suite 240, New York, NY 10011

Library of Congress Cataloging-in-Publication Data

Names: Porterfield, Jason, author.
Title: Marriage equality : Obergefell v. Hodges / Jason Porterfield.
Description: New York : Enslow Publishing, 2017. | Series: US Supreme
Court Landmark Cases | Includes bibliographical references and index.
Identifiers: LCCN 2016032317 | ISBN 9780766084360 (library bound)
Subjects: LCSH: Obergefell, James,—Trials, litigation, etc. | Same-sex marriage—Law and legislation—
United States—Cases. | Gay couples—Legal status, laws, etc.—United States—Cases. | Marriage law—
Untied States. | United States. Defense of Marriage Act. | California. Proposition 8 (2008)
Classification: LCC KF229.O24 P67 2017 | DDC 346.7301/68—dc23
LC record available at https://lccn.loc.gov/2016032317

Printed in Malaysia

To Our Readers: We have done our best to make sure all websites in this book were active and appropriate when we went to press. However, the author and the publisher have no control over and assume no liability for the material available on those websites or on any websites they may link to. Any comments or suggestions can be sent by e-mail to customerservice@enslow.com.

Contents

CHAPTER 1
Unequal in Ohio

On June 26, 2015, Jim Obergefell of Cincinnati, Ohio, was in Washington, DC. Like many Americans, he was anxiously awaiting the Supreme Court ruling that would decide whether or not to legalize same-sex marriage across the United States. In April, the Court had heard arguments from both sides of the issue. A ruling on the case was due in the early summer, but nobody knew the exact date it would be issued.

Supporters of same-sex marriage believed that the time had come for gay and lesbian couples across the country to be granted the dignity and legal rights bestowed by the institution of marriage. The movement had seen setbacks and intense opposition, but since Massachusetts had become the first state to legalize same-sex marriage in 2004, court victories had granted more rights to same-sex couples. In the 2013 case of *United States v. Windsor*, the US Supreme Court found that the federal government must recognize same-sex marriages.

Advocates believed that the reasoning behind the *Windsor* ruling would shortly be applied to the states.[1]

Opponents of same-sex marriage were also hopeful that the Supreme Court would resolve the issue, but they wanted to see state bans upheld. In their view, decisions over same-sex marriage belonged with the state legislatures and voters, not the courts. Many Americans still defined marriage as a union between a man and a woman for the purpose of procreation, or producing children. If state laws reflected this stance, the courts should not intervene. Opponents were encouraged by wording in *Windsor* that referenced the authority of the states in regulating domestic relations.

Obergefell's home state of Ohio was one of the states that refused to marry same-sex couples or recognize out-of-state same-sex marriage licenses, but Obergefell had a personal interest in this particular case before the Supreme Court. In 2013, he and his husband had filed a federal lawsuit asking that the state be required to recognize their marriage. After an appeals process and consolidation with several other cases, the landmark case of *Obergefell v. Hodges* reached the Supreme Court.

Finally, on that June morning in 2015, the Supreme Court handed down the decision that made same-sex marriage legal across the country. After hearing the ruling, Obergefell declared, "[T]he four words etched onto the front of the Supreme Court—'equal justice under law'— apply to us, too." But for Obergefell, it had been a long journey to victory.[2]

Protesters on both sides of the marriage equality issue hold signs outside the US Supreme Court building during the *Obergefell* hearing.

Finding Love

Jim Obergefell and John Arthur both attended college at the University of Cincinnati during the late 1980s and early 1990s. They didn't know each other then, but they had many friends in common. Obergefell (pronounced Oh-ber-guh-fell), a native of Sandusky, Ohio, graduated in 1992 and went on that fall to graduate school at Bowling Green State University. He often returned to Cincinnati for weekends. He and Arthur, a native of Chicago, Illinois, met twice while hanging out with mutual friends during one of those trips. They were friendly toward each other, but nothing more. They met for a third time on New Year's Eve of 1992 and fell in love.

After that third meeting, they became an inseparable couple. The attraction between them was so strong that Obergefell decided not to finish his graduate degree at Bowling Green. Obergefell had grown up in a Catholic household as the youngest of six children. He had come out to his family as gay, but Arthur was his first serious boyfriend. He moved back to Cincinnati to be with Arthur. They bought a home and started building a life together.

Like many places in the United States, Cincinnati had its share of people who didn't accept same-sex relationships or gay people in general. In 1993, voters passed an amendment to the city charter that banned the city from passing anti-discrimination laws designed to protect the rights of gay and lesbian people. Obergefell was active in trying to keep the amendment from passing. Twenty years would pass before he once again became an activist.[3]

Maryland Wedding

Obergefell and Arthur stayed together for those twenty years. They lived together as a couple in the Cincinnati area, where Obergefell built a real estate career and later became an information technology consultant. Arthur worked in benefits and project management for companies such as Macy's and Fidelity Investments. They traveled extensively and visited more than twenty countries together. The men wanted to get married, though same-sex marriage was illegal in Ohio and in most other places for much of their relationship. They thought about having a ceremony performed in a place where same-sex marriage was legal, but they wanted it to be more than a symbolic gesture. They didn't think it would mean anything until same-sex marriage was legal throughout the country.

In 2011, Arthur started having trouble walking. He was diagnosed with amyotrophic lateral sclerosis (ACL), often called Lou Gehrig's disease after the star baseball player whose career was cut short by the illness. People who have ACL lose their ability to move and even breathe. It is fatal, and there is no known cure.[4]

Obergefell became Arthur's caregiver as his partner's condition worsened. They started talking seriously about getting married. They wanted Arthur's death certificate to list him as "married," with Obergefell as his spouse. This would not happen as long as Ohio continued to ban same-sex marriages.

In 2013, the US Supreme Court ruled in the case of *United States v. Windsor*. The ruling struck down the federal ban on allowing same-sex married couples to receive the same federal marriage benefits as heterosexual couples. These benefits are extensive, and touch on everything from health care to taxes. Tax benefits for married people include the right to form a "family business" partnership with the spouse that allows business income to be divided. Married couples can also file joint tax returns.

In terms of estate planning, marriage benefits make it easier to inherit a portion of what a spouse leaves behind. They allow couples to receive tax exemptions from estate taxes and any gifts left to a spouse. Married couples can also make important decisions for their spouses, including medical and financial choices, should a husband or wife become incapable of making those decisions. Direct government benefits include the right to receive a spouse's Social Security, Medicare, or disability payments, the ability to receive his or her veterans' and military benefits, such as medical care, education options, and special loans, and the ability to receive a spouse's public assistance benefits, such as housing.

Employment benefits for married couples include the ability to receive coverage through a spouse's insurance plan, the right to take a family leave in order to help care for a sick spouse, taking bereavement time off if a spouse or a spouse's close relative dies, and being entitled to wages, worker's compensation benefits, and retirement plan benefits due after the death of a husband or wife. Medical benefits include being able to make medical decisions for one's spouse if he or she is unable to do so and being permitted to visit the spouse in a hospital's intensive care unit or other restricted area. The death benefits that were so important to Obergefell and Arthur provide the spouse with the right to make decisions regarding any post-death examinations and the right to make burial or funeral arrangements.

Married people receive family benefits which entitle them to file to become a stepparent, adopt their spouse's child, and apply for joint foster care rights. In the event of a divorce, they receive spousal or child support and visitation rights and the right to an even division of jointly-owned property. They can live in areas that are designated as being for families only, receive family rates for insurance, and get tuition discounts and other discounts.[5]

Obergefell and Arthur saw the *Windsor* ruling as opening the door to having same-sex marriage recognized by the state of Ohio. Arthur's health was getting worse, and they decided to go ahead and get married in one of the states where same-sex marriage was legal. Arthur needed constant medical care, so it had to be a state where Obergefell could make the arrangements on his own. They chose Maryland, which requires only one partner to be present to fill out paperwork for the marriage license. By that time, Arthur's health was so fragile that they weren't sure he would survive multiple trips. They hired a special medical plane to transport Arthur.[6] They flew into the Baltimore/Washington International Thurgood Marshall Airport Maryland on July 11, 2013. The ceremony took place inside the plane shortly after they landed. Arthur's aunt, Paulette Roberts, performed the ceremony. Officially and legally married, they promptly flew back to Cincinnati.[7]

Confusion in California

On November 4, 2008, California voters approved Proposition 8, which amended the state constitution to ban same-sex marriage. The ballot measure was highly contentious and expensive even before passage. Gay rights groups immediately filed a challenge that was heard before the state Supreme Court in 2009. The judges upheld the measure, but they also validated same-sex marriages that had been performed before the ban went into effect.

Challengers then moved to file a suit in federal court. In 2010, a San Francisco judge found Proposition 8 unconstitutional.

The state of California declined to appeal the ruling. In 2011, the California Supreme Court ruled that the proponents of Proposition 8 could file an appeal. The Ninth Circuit Court of Appeals upheld the earlier ruling, and the case of *Hollingsworth v. Perry* was granted a hearing in the US Supreme Court. Arguments were held on March 26, 2013, and the Court issued a decision on June 26, the same day that it ruled on the closely watched case of *United States v. Windsor*, which also examined the issue of same-sex marriage. The Court essentially declined to decide on Proposition 8, instead finding that the proponents did not have legal standing to defend the measure.[8]

As a result, the appeals court decision finding Proposition 8 unconstitutional remained in place. Within days, county clerks began issuing marriage licenses to same-sex couples. The circumstances and court actions surrounding California's Proposition 8 were a dramatic, high-stakes spectacle that ended with a victory for same-sex marriage in California, but the case did not ultimately decide the issue across the United States.

Legal Action

After the ceremony, Obergefell and Arthur faced another hurdle. Despite the fact that their marriage was legal in Maryland and in nine other states (and Washington, DC), Ohio still did not recognize same-sex marriages. They knew that Arthur did not have much time left, and they wanted the state to acknowledge their union.

They met with a Cincinnati attorney named Al Gerhardstein, who had been keeping track of developments since the *Windsor* ruling. Gerhardstein was looking for ways to use the *Windsor* ruling to push for widespread legal recognition of same-sex marriage. He set up a meeting with Obergefell and Arthur through a mutual friend. He explained to them that John Arthur's death certificate would still show him as single and would not mention Obergefell at all. He also told them that courts going back to the eighteenth century had repeatedly ruled that marriages were "portable," meaning that if a wedding was legal and valid in one state it would also be valid in another.[9]

Gerhardstein believed that Obergefell and Arthur had a strong case, and that they might be able to overturn Ohio's ban on same-sex marriages. He offered to act as their attorney if they decided to take legal action. Obergefell and Arthur had not gotten married in order to become activists or to make a statement. They had flown to Maryland at great cost and held a ceremony because they loved each other deeply and wanted that love to be legally recognized. Gerhardstein impressed them with his intelligence, his kindness, and his interest in human rights. They agreed to let him represent them in court.[10]

Gerhardstein filed a federal lawsuit on behalf of Obergefell and Arthur on July 19, 2013, just over a week after their wedding. It was the first legal challenge to a marriage ban since the *Windsor* ruling. Gerhardstein wanted his clients to win their case, so he focused on a very narrow part of the law that challenged the portion of the Ohio marriage ban that stated same-sex marriages performed in other states would not be considered legal.

Gerhardstein, Obergefell, and Arthur believed their case would serve as another small step for marriage equality.

Ohio's governor, John Kasich, was named as the lead defendant in the case. Also named as defendants were Attorney General Mike DeWine and the Registrar of the City of Cincinnati Health Department, Office of Vital Records, Dr. Camille Jones. Jones was included in the case because her office was responsible for issuing death certificates.

The suit was filed in the United States District Court for the Southern District of Ohio, with the plaintiffs seeking "declaratory and injunctive relief"[11] that would force the state to recognize their marriage. In light of Arthur's delicate health as he neared the end of his life, Gerhardstein also sought to put a restraining order in place that would bar the state from issuing a death certificate that didn't recognize his marriage. On July 21, 2013, Judge Timothy Black agreed and put a temporary restraining order in place until the case could be decided, citing Ohio's history of recognizing out of state marriages for death certificates.[12] Doing otherwise would be discriminatory and unconstitutional, and therefore not in the state's interest. It was a small victory in what would become a much more important case than the plaintiffs had expected.[13]

CHAPTER 2

Marriage in the United States

In the United States, marriage laws are decided by individual states. These laws govern who can get married, who can perform the ceremony, and what fees or requirements must be met—such as licenses. A marriage that takes place in one state is almost always considered valid in others. However, marriage between two people of the same sex was not legal in any state until the twenty-first century. Gay and lesbian people have long been discriminated against in other ways as well.

Legacies of Intolerance

For centuries, homosexuality was viewed as abnormal and morally wrong. People who loved or were attracted to members of the same gender were often outcasts or had to hide their feelings. Otherwise, they might risk exile, jail, or institutionalization. In some places, they might face torture or even execution.[1]

In the United States prior to 1962, it was a felony in every state to have a sexual relationship with another person of the same sex. Homosexuality was largely viewed as either a moral failing or a psychological problem. Many gay people hid their relationships out of fear of being discovered. In a country where discrimination based on race and gender was often the norm, losing their jobs, their homes, and even their families was a very real possibility. They may have been open with their close friends and family, but even that was a risk.[2]

Even immigration was affected by anti-gay prejudice. The Immigration Act of 1917 banned lesbian and gay people from moving to the United States, as well as people from Asia, and "psychopaths, inferiors, and people with abnormal sexual instincts."[3] The Immigration Act of 1965 removed all immigration quotas based on race, religion, and nationality. However, the law labeled lesbian and gay people as "sexual deviants" and banned them outright.[4] The ban on gay and lesbian immigration loosened in 1980 and was finally eliminated in 1990.

Attitudes toward homosexuality in general began shifting during the latter part of the twentieth century. The changes to immigration law were not the only signs of progress for the gay and lesbian community. Activist groups began pushing back against discrimination against lesbian, gay, bisexual, and transgender (LGBT) people. States began doing away with their laws against homosexuality during the 1970s, and stopped treating it as a psychological condition. The last of those laws were ruled unconstitutional in the *Lawrence v. Texas* ruling in 2003.[5] Society in general gradually became more tolerant through the work of advocacy groups and their allies.

The lawyers Ruth Harlow and Paul Smith talk to the press after the Supreme Court hears arguments in the *Lawrence v. Texas* case. There were many protesters present during the hearings.

However, stereotypes about LGBT people have persisted, as has discrimination. Every time a comedian gets attention for telling a tasteless and insensitive joke or a professional athlete uses an anti-gay slur on the field, it serves as a reminder that bigotry against the LGBT community is still very much a fact of life. Some places still allow outright discrimination against LGBT people in terms of jobs, housing, or business dealings. In extreme cases, this intolerance even manifests itself in acts of violence.

Baker v. Nelson

Decades before same-sex marriage became a reality in some states and a passionately debated topic across the nation, the 1972 case of *Baker v. Nelson* had quietly established precedent on the issue.

In 1971, during the early days of the gay rights movement, the same-sex couple of Richard John Baker and James Michael McConnell applied for a marriage license in Minnesota. Upon being rejected, they appealed to the state Supreme Court. Their grounds were ahead of their time—the claim stated that they "are deprived of liberty and property without due process and are denied the equal protection of the laws, both guaranteed by the Fourteenth Amendment" due to prohibition of same-sex marriages.

The judge affirmed the earlier dismissal, stating, "The institution of marriage as a union of man and woman, uniquely involving the procreation and rearing of children within a family, is as old as the book of Genesis."[6] The argument concerning procreation and marriage would also be repeated in future court cases. Later in 1972, the Supreme Court declined to hear the case in a terse rejection: "Appeal from Sup. Ct. Minn. dismissed for want of substantial federal question."[7]

Legal opponents of same-sex marriage would widely cite the case of *Baker v. Nelson* in their arguments. Many court rulings, however, gave the precedent scant notice, perhaps because the case was not discussed before the Supreme Court. The decision of *Obergefell v. Hodges* of 2015 explicitly overruled the *Baker* finding.

Spotlight on Marriage

The movement to grant gay and lesbian couples the right to marry began gaining more attention in the early 1990s, and more traction. More setbacks followed *Baker v. Nelson*. For example, in 1973, Maryland became the first state to pass a law banning marriages between people of the same sex.[8] There were also major gains, such as the passage of the nation's first domestic partnership law—in Berkeley, California—in 1984,[9] and the first mass same-sex wedding ceremony, held in Washington, DC, in 1987 and featuring some 2,000 gay and lesbian couples.[10]

One of the most significant signs of progress was a 1989 ruling by the New York State Court of Appeals, in which the court decided that a same-sex couple living together for more than ten years qualified as a family. The ruling allowed Miguel Braschi to remain in the rent-controlled New York City apartment he had lived in with his partner, Leslie Blanchard, until Blanchard's death in 1986. Under the city's rent-control guidelines, a landlord could not legally evict a living spouse or other relative who had been living with the deceased tenant. It marked the first time that a state's highest court had ever recognized an LGBT couple as a family.[11] That same year, the State Bar of California urged recognition of same-sex marriage.[12]

The year 1993 was a watershed year for both sides of the same-sex marriage debate. That year, the Supreme Court of Hawaii ruled in the case of *Baehr v. Miike* that the state had to present compelling evidence that same-sex marriages should be banned.[13] Three same-sex couples had applied for marriage licenses in 1990 through the Hawaii Department of Health. They argued that they met all of the state's requirements for receiving marriage licenses. The head of the department had asked the Hawaii Attorney General's Office for an opinion regarding whether a license could be issued, and the office ruled that the fundamental right to marriage applied only to heterosexual couples. The applications were denied, and the couples sued.[14]

The case came before Judge Kevin S. C. Chang in 1996. The state argued that limiting marriage to heterosexual couples was necessary for five reasons, those being:

a. That the State has a compelling interest in protecting the health and welfare of children and other persons. ...

b. That the State has a compelling interest in fostering procreation within a marital setting. ...

c. That the State has a compelling interest in securing or assuring recognition of Hawaii marriages in other jurisdictions. ...

d. That the State has a compelling interest in protecting the State's public fisc from the reasonably foreseeable effects of State approval of same-sex marriage in the laws of Hawaii. ...

e. That the State has a compelling state interest in protecting civil liberties, including the reasonably foreseeable effects of State approval of same-sex marriages, on its citizens.[15]

Judge Chang determined that the state had not proven that a ban on same-sex marriage was necessary. He called the ban unconstitutional and ordered the state to begin issuing licenses to gay and lesbian couples. Chang cited testimony given by experts that same-sex couples could be good parents and rejected the state's argument that banning same-sex marriages was necessary in order to protect children. His order to issue licenses was put on hold while the state appealed.[16]

Though the case was a victory, it touched off a flurry of action by lawmakers who opposed same-sex marriage. At the time that *Baehr v. Miike* was making its way through the courts, there was strong opposition to same-sex marriage in many parts of the United States. There had been some progress in the way that gay and lesbian people were treated and viewed. Marriage, however, was too great a step for many to take.[17]

Opponents to same-sex marriage used (and continue to use) many of the same arguments that the state of Hawaii brought. Among their reasons were the belief that gay and lesbian couples did not make good parents, that their lifestyles were immoral or "wrong," and that same-sex marriage somehow violates the sanctity of marriage. Some opponents also cite religious objections, in the belief that homosexuality is a sin against God and that allowing same-sex marriage is the same as taking part in that sin. These opponents organized powerful lobbying campaigns to pressure Hawaii's lawmakers to find a way to block same-sex marriages. They also pressured politicians in their own states to pass laws to bar same-sex couples from marrying.[18]

Hawaii appealed the ruling, sending the case back to the Supreme Court of Hawaii. Opponents of same-sex marriage in Hawaii acted to prevent what they feared would be a flood of same-sex couples from other states. Opponents in the rest of the United States feared that they would also be legally bound to recognize same-sex marriages performed in Hawaii. Those states began passing laws that forbade marriages that were not between a man and a woman. Thirty states would eventually pass laws or approve constitutional amendments banning same-sex marriages or civil unions (legally binding arrangements offered by states that provide some of the same protections as marriage).[19]

In November 1998, Hawaii voters passed an amendment to the state constitution that explicitly gave the state the right to reserve marriage for heterosexual couples only. In 1999, the Supreme Court of Hawaii ruled that the amendment removed the plaintiffs' objections regarding the legal requirements for marriage. Since the state constitution had been amended to say that marriage could exist only between a man and a woman, they no longer met all of those requirements.[20]

The Defense of Marriage Act

The most significant reaction to the 1993 *Baehr v. Miike* ruling came from the US Congress. In 1996, A Republican member of the US House of Representatives from Georgia named Bob Barr wrote a bill called the Defense of Marriage Act (DOMA). Barr's bill was designed to allow states to refuse to acknowledge same-sex marriages that were performed in other states. It also limited marriage benefits so that only heterosexual couples would be entitled to tax breaks, survivor benefits, veterans' benefits, and other privileges otherwise guaranteed by law through marriage.[21]

Unlike many bills introduced in Congress, DOMA was short—only two pages long. It formally defined marriage as a relationship between husband and wife:

In determining the meaning of any Act of Congress, or of any ruling, regulation, or interpretation of the various administrative bureaus and agencies of the United States, the word 'marriage' means only a legal union between one man and one woman as husband and wife, and the word 'spouse' refers only to a person of the opposite sex who is a husband or a wife.[22]

Barr introduced DOMA in the House of Representatives on May 7, 1996. Don Nickles, a Republican from Oklahoma, sponsored the bill in the Senate.[23] The bill found overwhelming support from members of both the Republican and the Democratic parties in both chambers of Congress. While addressing Congress about the bill, Barr told his fellow representatives, "The very foundations of our society are in danger of being burned."[24]

The 435-member house passed the bill with an overwhelming vote of 342-67. Two representatives voted "present"–meaning they wanted the record to show that they were there but chose not vote yes or no. Twenty-two did not vote.[25] The bill passed in the 100-member Senate by a margin of 85 in favor and 14 against, with one senator not voting.[26] Despite the bipartisan vote, it was a partisan issue. Only one Republican in the House of Representatives voted against the bill, and all fourteen Senate votes against it came from Democrats. Those voting in favor of the bill included many politicians who would later support same-sex marriage. Even Bob Barr, the bill's author, eventually campaigned against DOMA.[27]

The bill had enough support in both chambers of Congress that its supporters would be able to override a presidential veto—a procedure in which the president declines to sign a bill into law and sends it back to Congress with language explaining why it was rejected.

Rather than face criticism from supporters of the bill while he was running for reelection, President Bill Clinton signed DOMA into law on September 20, 1996, ten days after it was passed in the Senate. Clinton had been viewed as an ally to the LGBT community, but he was criticized by the bill's opponents for signing it. However, he did not hold a public signing ceremony or give a speech for the bill, choosing to sign it after midnight. In his brief written statement about DOMA, he urged Congress to also pass the Employment Non-Discrimination Act (ENDA), a proposed law that would make it illegal to discriminate against lesbian and gay people in the workplace. Unlike DOMA, ENDA has often been discussed but has never become law.[28]

Massachusetts Verdict

The passage of DOMA slowed efforts to make same-sex marriage legal. Some states moved quickly to pass their own laws to define marriage as between a man and a woman only. By 2001, forty-one states had passed laws or constitutional amendments to deny same-sex couples the right to marry or to be recognized as married.[29] Despite the continuing backlash against *Baehr v. Miike*, there were a few victories for same-sex marriage supporters.

In 1997, Hawaii passed a "reciprocal beneficiary" law that grants couples who are blocked by law from marrying access to some legal rights at the state level.[30] California passed a domestic partner law in 1999 that offered some legal protections to same-sex couples, and in 2000 Vermont passed the first civil union law in the United States.[31]

In 2003, the Massachusetts Supreme Court heard the case *Goodridge v. Department of Public Health*.[32] The case began in 2001, when the organization GLBTQ Legal Advocates and Defenders (GLAD) sued the Massachusetts Department of Public Health on behalf of seven gay and lesbian couples who had been denied marriage licenses. The plaintiffs were all in long-term relationships, and four of the couples were raising children.[33]

On November 18, 2003, the court ruled 4-3 that denying the licenses violated the state constitution's guarantees of liberty and equality, and did not serve the interests of the state.[34] In the majority opinion, the justices stated: "We declare that barring an individual from the protections, benefits, and obligations of civil marriage solely because that person would marry a person of the same sex violates the Massachusetts Constitution."[35]

The decision marked the first time a state's highest court had found that same-sex couples should have the right to marry.[36] The initial *Baehr v. Miike* rulings had only questioned the state's right to deny licenses, and that right was ultimately upheld. The decision also had popular support in Massachusetts, with 50 percent of those polled by the *Boston Globe* and WBZ-TV saying that they agreed with the ruling to 38 percent opposing it. 11 percent had no opinion. In the same poll, conducted just days after the ruling, 53 percent of those questioned said that they were against changing the state constitution to ban same-sex marriage.[37]

The court stayed the decision for 180 days while opponents looked for a way to either get the ruling overturned, amend the constitution, or find some other way to prevent the state from issuing same-sex licenses. The governor at the time, Mitt Romney, called for amending the state constitution to ban same-sex marriages. Opponents outside of Massachusetts were also vocal, and even President George W. Bush suggested adding a "marriage amendment" to the US Constitution that would ban same-sex marriages. They were ultimately unsuccessful, and the state started issuing licenses to lesbian and gay couples on May 17, 2004.[38]

More than 6,100 same-sex couples were married in Massachusetts by the end of 2004 and more than 25,000 by the end of 2013. Other states followed suit, and by 2013 twelve states and Washington, DC, allowed same-sex marriage.[39]

As significant as the *Goodridge* decision was, the 2013 US Supreme Court ruling *United States v. Windsor* opened the door even wider for same-sex marriage. The case centered around a lesbian couple, Edith Windsor and Thea Spyer, who were married in Canada in 2007—Canada legalized same-sex marriage in 2005. Spyer died in 2009, and Windsor sought to claim her estate tax exemption for surviving spouses. Due to the Defense of Marriage Act's prohibition against same-sex spouses claiming federal benefits, the Internal Revenue Service denied her claim and forced her to pay more than $360,000 in estate taxes.[40]

Edith Windsor was eighty-three during the *United States v. Windsor* hearing. She had been with her partner, Thea Spyer, for forty-two years when Spyer died.

Windsor filed a lawsuit against the federal government on November 9, 2010, through attorney Roberta Kaplan and with support from the American Civil Liberties Union (ACLU).[41]

She sought to have the money refunded, based on the argument that DOMA unfairly singled out legally married gay and lesbian couples for treatment that was different from other couples in similar situations. Specifically, the suit challenged the constitutionality of Section 3 of DOMA, which stated:

In determining the meaning of any Act of Congress, or of any ruling, regulation, or interpretation of the various administrative bureaus and agencies of the United States, the word 'marriage' means only a legal union between one man and one woman as husband and wife, and the word 'spouse' refers only to a person of the opposite sex who is a husband or a wife.[42]

In February 2011, US Attorney General Eric Holder announced that the Department of Justice would not defend Section 3 of DOMA. Windsor's suit proceeded, with the US House of Representatives' Bipartisan Legal Advisory Group (BLAG) defending the act's constitutionality. The case reached the US Supreme Court in March 2013. On June 26, 2013, the court ruled 5-4 that Section 3 was unconstitutional.[43]

The Windsor ruling touched off strong reactions from both sides of the marriage debate. Opponents of same-sex marriage viewed it as an overreach by the court. Supporters saw it as a victory that could lead to the legalization of same-sex marriage throughout the United States. In fact, many cities and states used the ruling to pass laws permitting same-sex marriage.

CHAPTER 3

A Growing Case

Obergefell and Arthur's case soon attracted national attention. The *Windsor* ruling was viewed by many as a signal that the court might be moving toward a more direct ruling in favor of same sex marriage. Several other suits seeking to overturn bans against same-sex marriage were active at that time.

District Court

Obergefell and Arthur's case against the State of Ohio received its first hearing in the United States District Court for the Southern District of Ohio. District courts are part of the federal court system, which also includes circuit courts and the US Supreme Court.

There is at least one US district court in each state, and more than one in most. In all, there are 89 district courts in the 50 states and 94 total, counting those in the territories.[1]

Supporters of same-sex marriage stand outside the Potter Stewart Courthouse in Ohio, where the judges would decide whether same-sex marriage should be recognized for several couples, including Obergefell and Arthur.

District courts are often called the workhorse courts of the judicial system due to the high number of cases they hear. The district courts handle both criminal cases and civil cases—a civil case is one in which a person or group feels wronged by another and sues, while criminal cases deal with accused lawbreakers. Different judges handle different types of cases under these classifications.[2]

The federal district courts have limited jurisdiction over civil cases, meaning that they only hear cases that are authorized by federal laws or by the Constitution. Plaintiffs in civil court cases ask for either monetary relief—a cash payment to correct a situation—or equitable relief, in which the defendant is ordered to do or not do something.[3] With their case, Obergefell and Arthur wanted Ohio's law against recognizing same-sex marriages to be judged a violation of their rights and pleaded for its enforcement to end.

The loser of a civil district court case can appeal the outcome through a district court of appeals, which are also called circuit courts. Each district court is part of one of eleven court circuits within the federal court system. Each circuit covers several states.[4] The US District Court for the Southern District of Ohio is part of the Sixth Circuit, which also includes Michigan, Tennessee, and Kentucky. The court of appeals can either uphold or strike down the lower court's ruling. Any appeal to a court of appeals ruling would go to the US Supreme Court, which decides whether or not to hear that appeal. If the Supreme Court does take the matter up, its ruling can set a precedent for how similar cases are interpreted. If the court declines to hear the case, the decision by the court of appeals is allowed to stand.[5]

US district court judges, as well as court of appeals judges and Supreme Court justices, are nominated by the president and must be confirmed by the United States Senate. They are appointed for a life term. There are no formal qualifications for becoming a judge, but most federal judges distinguish themselves in the field of law before being considered, either as a lower court judge or in private practice or academia. Four district court judges heard cases that were eventually consolidated into *Obergefell v. Hodges*. Judge Timothy Black was nominated by President Barack Obama and began his judgeship in Ohio in 2010. Judge Bernard A. Friedman, nominated by President Ronald Reagan, had served as a federal judge in Michigan since 1988.

Judge John G. Heyburn II, nominated by President George H. W. Bush, had served as a federal judge in Kentucky since 1992. Aleta A. Trauger, nominated by President Bill Clinton, had served as a federal judge in Tennessee since 1998.[6] In the early 2010s, these US district judges would all bring their expertise and long experience to the issue of same-sex marriage.

The Ohio Decision

Obergefell and Arthur's case in district court held some urgency for the couple, considering Arthur's poor health. The restraining order granted by Justice Timothy Black protected the couple from the issuance of a death certificate listing Arthur as unmarried. Arthur died on Oct. 22, 2013.[7]

Obergefell carried on with the suit, which had been amended to remove the governor and attorney general as defendants. Meanwhile, the case began to grow in scope and momentum as more plaintiffs filed suits challenging Ohio's refusal to recognize same-sex marriages.

David Michener and William Ives were committed partners who were raising three adopted children together in Cincinnati, Ohio. They had been together for eighteen years when they married in July 2013 in Delaware, where they owned a second home. The state of Delaware had recently legalized same-sex marriage. Less than two months later, however, Ives died unexpectedly of natural causes in Cincinnati at the age of fifty-four. Like Obergefell, Michener wanted his husband's death certificate to recognize their marriage and acknowledge him as

Ives' surviving spouse. In September 2013, he decided to join Obergefell's suit. As with Arthur, the court issued an order that his death certificate acknowledge his out-of-state marriage.[8]

Robert Grunn, the owner of the Cincinnati funeral home that served Obergefell, also joined the case. As a licensed funeral director, Grunn was responsible for listing information on death certificates—documents that are important for survivors administering wills and inheriting property. As a gay man himself, he wanted to have the legal right to recognize same-sex marriages and the benefits conferred. He announced that he planned to recognize future out-of-state same-sex marriages in violation of Ohio's law and risk being prosecuted.[9]

The amended suit, which now listed Obergefell, Michener, and Grunn as co-plaintiffs, was filed on September 26, 2013.[10] Named as defendants were Dr. Camille Jones, Registrar of the City of Cincinnati Health Department, Office of Vital Records, and Dr. Theodore Wymyslo, Director of the Ohio Department of Health. In October, the defendants moved to have the case dismissed on the grounds that any controversy had been settled with Arthur's death. Since the relevant death certificates recognized their marriages and named their surviving spouses, didn't that mean that the matter had been resolved? The defendant argued that Grunn had no legal basis for challenging the law.[11]

Judge Black rejected the move for dismissal. He found that Grunn's claims were valid in that he did face a genuine threat of criminal prosecution if he chose to recognize same-sex marriages on death certificates. The claim also involved his personal and professional responsibility, since his future clients were likely to rely on him to be responsive to their concerns, including matters regarding their constitutional rights. In addition, considering the growth of the number of states in which same-sex marriage was legal, the time was "ripe" for a challenge to Ohio's law. The judge thought it highly probable that repercussions for Grunn recognizing out-of-state same-sex marriages would arise in the near future—it was not some unlikely, distant prospect.[12]

Obergefell v. Wymyslo continued to work its way through the legal system. On December 18, oral arguments were heard before Judge Black in the US District Court.[13]

On December 23, 2013, Judge Black ruled that Ohio must recognize out-of-state same-sex marriages on death certificates.[14] He found that Ohio's refusal to recognize these marriages was unconstitutional on grounds concerning due process and equal protection:

> Under the Constitution of the United States, Ohio must recognize valid out-of-state marriages between same-sex couples on Ohio death certificates, just as Ohio recognizes all other out-of-state marriages, if valid in the state performed ...
>
> [O]nce you get married lawfully in one state, another state cannot summarily take your marriage away, because the right to remain married is properly recognized as a fundamental liberty interest protected by the Due Process Clause of the United States Constitution.
>
> Moreover, as this Court held in its initial Orders this summer and reaffirms today, by treating lawful same-sex marriages differently than it treats lawful opposite sex marriages

(e. g., marriages of first cousins, marriages of certain minors, and common law marriages), Ohio law, as applied to these Plaintiffs, violates the United States Constitution's guarantee of equal protection: "No State shall make or enforce any law which shall ... deny to any person within its jurisdiction equal protection of the laws."[14]

This line of reasoning, citing these constitutional grounds, would be mentioned again and again in rulings confirming marriage equality.

The Fourteenth Amendment and Civil Rights

The Fourteenth Amendment to the US Constitution was ratified in 1868 in the aftermath of the Civil War. The Amendment consists of five parts: the Citizenship Clause, the Privileges and Immunities Clause, the Due Process Clause, the Equal Protection Clause, and the Enforcement Clause. (A clause is a section within a legal document.) At the time, many states were still attempting to curtail the rights of former slaves. The Fourteenth Amendment placed certain restrictions on state powers and granted all citizens key rights and protections. It dramatically expanded civil rights at the time, and it has been applied in many landmark cases in the twentieth and twenty-first centuries. The Supreme Court has often used the Fourteenth Amendment to extend the provisions in the Bill of Rights to state law.[15]

The Equal Protection Clause in particular has been used to expand the civil rights of various groups. It requires that all people in a state be treated equally under the law, thereby prohibiting discrimination on the basis of status such as race, national origin, or gender. Such groups are categorized as "suspect classifications," which provides certain legal protections against discrimination. Sexual orientation, however, has not been ruled a "suspect classification."[16]

The judge also stated that the defendants had not presented any evidence that demonstrated that recognizing same-sex marriages harmed state interest. Rather, it served to stigmatize same-sex married couples.[17]

This was a limited ruling, meaning that it only applied in a narrow set of circumstances. The judge specified that his decision addressed the matter of death certificates, and recognition on death certificates is only one of many benefits conferred by marriage. The ruling did not seek to expand the recognition of rights bestowed by same-sex marriage beyond death certificates.[18]

Nonetheless, the ruling established a new precedent with its requirement that Ohio recognize out-of-state same-sex marriages. Judge Black's broad reasoning could be applied in the future to other circumstances under which marriage conferred benefits. He heavily cited the *Windsor* ruling in his findings, which had required that the federal government recognize same-sex marriages. *Obergefell v. Wymyslo* extended the same rationale to the state level.[19]

On January 24, 2014, the defendant appealed the case to the Sixth Circuit Court of Appeals. As the appeal process began, the defendant listed in the case changed. Dr. Wymyslo resigned from his position at the Ohio Department of Health, replaced by Interim Director Lance Himes. In August 2014,

Richard Hodges was appointed Director of the Ohio Department of Health. The case then became "*Obergefell v. Hodges*," and this was the designation that would reach the Supreme Court.[20]

Adding Cases

Obergefell was not alone in challenging state law banning same-sex marriage. A flurry of litigation over marriage equality was taking place across the country.

Shortly after the *Obergefell v. Wymyslo* ruling, a group of couples in Ohio filed another lawsuit over the state's refusal to recognize same-sex marriages. The case, *Henry v. Himes* (later *Henry v. Hodges*), was brought by Brittani Henry and Brittni Rogers, a same-sex couple who was in a long-term relationship before being married in New York in 2014. The couple wanted to start a family, and Henry became pregnant.[21] By Ohio law, only Henry could be listed as the baby's parent on the birth certificate. Henry was joined in the lawsuit by two other Ohio same-sex couples in similar circumstances, along with a married same-sex New York couple who had adopted a baby in Ohio. Their adoption agency also participated in the suit, objecting to Ohio law that refused to list both spouses as parents.[22]

The plaintiff's challenge was broader than that of the *Obergefell v. Wymyslo* case. They sought to have Ohio's ban on recognition of out-of-state same-sex marriages entirely struck down.

On April 14, 2014, Judge Black ruled in their favor. He instructed that both spouses' names be listed on their children's birth certificates. More broadly, he found that Ohio's ban on

Here Brittani Henry and Brittni Rogers are shown with their daughter, while Rogers holds up the birth certificate that lists both of them as her parents.

recognizing out-of-state same-sex marriages was unconstitutional. Shortly afterward, he granted a stay on his decision while the state appealed the ruling, meaning that Ohio was not required to take any action to comply with the ruling until the appeal was completed.[23]

Other states that fell within the Sixth Circuit were also grappling with legal cases involving same-sex marriage. In Michigan, a lawsuit was brought by April DeBoer and Jane Rowse, an unmarried same-sex couple, who were both foster parents of three children. DeBoer legally adopted one of the children and Rowse the other two, but they could not hold joint adoption. In 2012, they filed legal action seeking to change the adoption code.[24]

The Court noted that it was not the adoption code that prevented joint adoption—it was the state's constitutional amendment banning gay marriage. The plaintiffs amended their lawsuit to challenge the constitutional amendment. Judge Bernard A. Friedman then chose to wait to continue with the case until *United States v. Windsor* had been decided. The trial began in February of 2014. Proceedings lasted for nine days, with both sides calling expert witnesses who weighed in on whether or not children fared better when raised by opposite-sex parents. On March 21, 2014, Judge Friedman issued a ruling that found the amendment prohibiting gay marriage to be unconstitutional.[25] The US Court of Appeals for the Sixth Circuit quickly placed a hold on the decision, although not before hundreds of same-sex Michigan couples obtained marriage licenses.[26]

In Kentucky, the case *Bourke v. Beshear* challenged the state's laws banning recognition of out-of-state same-sex marriage and excluding same-sex couples from the benefits of marriage. Gregory Bourke and Michael DeLeon of Louisville had been together for thirty-one years and were raising two adopted teenage children, who were also named in the lawsuit. The couple married in Canada in 2004. They were joined in the challenge, filed in late 2013, by three other married same-sex couples in similar circumstances. The defendant listed in the case was Steve Beshear, governor of Kentucky. On February 12, 2014, US District Judge John G. Heyburn II ruled that Kentucky's law denying recognition of same-sex marriages was unconstitutional.[27]

A follow-up case to *Bourke v. Beshear* was filed on February 14, 2014. Timothy Love and Lawrence Ysunza asked to intervene in the lawsuit on the basis that the broad arguments of Bourke applied to their circumstances. The Louisville couple had been together for thirty-four years when they applied for a marriage certificate in 2014, which was refused. They held that denying them the right to marry discriminated against them and denied them significant benefits granted by marriage, such as the right to make health decisions for the other in case of emergency. They were joined by another same-sex couple that had also been refused a marriage certificate.[28]

Judge Heyburn allowed the intervention, with the new case of *Love v. Beshear* challenging the constitutionality of Kentucky's ban on same-sex marriage. On July 1, 2014, Judge Heyburn found that the ban was indeed unconstitutional. As in *Bourke*, he found that it violated the plaintiffs' right to equal protection. Stays were placed on both findings pending appeal.[29]

In Tennessee, Valeria Tanco and Sophy Jesty challenged state laws that failed to recognize their out-of-state same-sex marriage. The women had married in New York before moving to pursue careers in Tennessee, and Tanco was expecting their first child at the time of the lawsuit. Recognition of their marriage would provide many benefits to them, such as legal acknowledgement of Jesty as a parent and the rights to co-own property and qualify for a family health insurance plan. They were joined by two other same-sex couples in similar circumstances (a fourth couple dropped out of the suit) when they filed a case against Bill Haslam, governor of Tennessee, in late 2013. On March 14, 2014, District Court Judge Aleta A. Trauger issued a preliminary injunction in *Tanco v. Haslam* ordering the defendants to recognize the plaintiff's marriages. She cited both *Obergefell* and *Bourke* in a footnote and predicted that "proscriptions against same-sex marriage will soon become a footnote in the annals of American history" on constitutional grounds.[30]

CHAPTER 4

A Setback in Court

A ttorneys for the states filed appeals of the verdicts overturning the bans on same-sex marriage. On April 25, 2014, the Sixth Circuit Court of Appeals decided to take up the appeals and ordered that a panel of judges be appointed to hear them as soon as possible. The cases were heard separately, though some were combined as a way to simplify the hearing process. The Ohio cases were consolidated into one. Michener and Grunn had been added as plaintiffs in September 2013, and *Henry v. Wymyslo* was consolidated with *Obergefell v. Hodges* in May 2014 for purposes of argument. The Kentucky cases were consolidated under *Bourke v. Beshear* in July 2014. *DeBoer v. Snyder* and *Tanco v. Haslam* would be heard on their own.[1]

The weeks before the cases were heard were tense for both supporters and opponents of same-sex marriage. On the pro-equality side, there was excitement that lesbian and gay couples might finally have their marriages recognized and that unmarried couples might be able to have weddings in their home states. Those who opposed same-sex marriage dreaded the possibility of the courts intervening in what they saw as the right of each state and its voters to decide the matter.

The Courts of Appeals

The Sixth Circuit Court of Appeals, located in Cincinnati, Ohio, covers that state along with Michigan, Kentucky, and Tennessee. As one of eleven such appeals courts in the nation, it holds a great deal of influence in upholding or striking down state laws within its territories. Most cases that make it out of the district courts are decided at the appeals court level. The US Supreme Court hears less than 1 percent of cases filed, meaning that the courts of appeals generally give the final rulings in the cases that come before them.[2]

The three judges who would hear the appeals filed in *Obergefell* and its related cases would be examining lower court trials that happened in four different states: Ohio, Tennessee, Michigan, and Kentucky. Two of the appeals court justices, Deborah L. Cook and Jeffrey S. Sutton, were from Ohio. The third, Martha Craig Daughtrey, came from Tennessee.

Cook was a state appellate judge on the Ohio Ninth District Court of Appeals and was twice elected to serve as a justice of the Ohio Supreme Court. She was first nominated to the Sixth Circuit by President George W. Bush in May 2001 and confirmed by the US Senate in May 2003.[3] Sutton was a former state solicitor who had once been a law clerk for US Supreme Court justices Antonin Scalia and Lewis Powell and taught law at the Ohio State University College of Law. He was also nominated to the Sixth Circuit by President George W. Bush in May 2001 and joined the court in April 2003.[4] Daughtrey was nominated to the circuit in 1993 by President Bill Clinton and joined the court later that year. Prior to that, she was the first woman to serve as an assistant US attorney for the Middle District of Tennessee.[5]

Filing the Appeal

Wymyslo filed the appeal in *Obergefell v. Wymyslo* on January 16, 2014. On March 18, the governor of Tennessee appealed the *Tanco v. Haslam* decision, followed by *Bourke v. Beshear* on the same day, *DeBoer v. Snyder* on March 21, *Henry v. Himes* on May 9, and *Love v. Beshear* on July 8.

The appellant brief in *Obergefell v. Wymyslo* was filed on April 10, 2014, and Obergefell's appellee brief was filed on April 24. Appellant and respondent briefs were also filed in the other cases. After consolidation, the cases that were to be heard by the Sixth District Court of Appeals were *Obergefell v. Hodges, Tanco v. Haslam, DeBoer v. Snyder,* and *Bourke v. Beshear.* Because of the large number of couples waiting on the ruling, the court set expedited briefing schedules in some of the cases, cutting the time for the appellants and appellees to file briefs.

Here April DeBoer and Jayne Rowse hold a press conference with their lawyer Carole Stanyar (in the pink shirt) after the *DeBoer v. Snyder* hearing.

The Oral Arguments

Oral arguments in the cases were scheduled for August 6, 2014. The attention attracted by the case brought people from all four states to the courtroom in Cincinnati to show their support for one side or the other. Opponents and supporters of same-sex marriage held protests outside the courthouse the day before. An overflow room was set aside for people who could not get in to the courtroom, and video screens were provided so they could watch the proceedings. People arrived at the courthouse hours before the trial to find seats.[6]

Attorneys in each case would present their positions, and the judges would rule on the cases as a whole. In the case of *DeBoer v. Snyder*, oral arguments took about an hour. Michigan Solicitor General Aaron Lindstrom argued that the case wasn't as much about whether or not same-sex marriage should be legal, but about who should get to make the decision. Lindstrom's position was that the states themselves should have the right to decide, rather than federal judges. He argued that the case was not about the definition of marriage, but about who gets to define it.[7]

"Because the US Constitution is silent about how to define marriage, the issue remains where it has always been: with the people," he argued. "When people of good will disagree—and they invariably do—they should engage in compassionate and civil dialogue in the public square."[8]

Attorney Carole Stanyar, representing DeBoer, argued that the bans on same-sex marriage violated the Fourteenth Amendment to the Constitution, as did the US Supreme Court's verdict in *Baker v. Nelson*.

"As a result of the decision below, gay and lesbian citizens in Michigan, Ohio, Kentucky and Tennessee are denied the fundamental freedom and equal right to marry," Stanyar stated. "Their families – including their children – are deprived of the status, dignity, security, stability and myriad material and legal protections that marriage brings. This Court should hold that prohibiting same-sex couples from marrying violates our nation's most cherished and essential guarantees."[9]

In *Obergefell v. Himes*, Ohio Solicitor General Eric Murphy argued that the District Court had overstepped its bounds by striking down the state's ban on same-sex marriage. Murphy, like Lindstrom, steered his argument away from the question of whether or not same-sex marriage should be legal, focusing instead on who should make that distinction. Murphy said that there was no deeply-rooted right to same-sex marriage, and that no one knew what impact allowing gay marriage might have on children. "In rejecting the Ohio voters' decision on this public policy issue, the District Court ignored its place in the Judicial hierarchy and our constitutional democracy," Murphy said.[10]

Speaking on behalf of Obergefell and Henry, attorney Al Gehardstein pointed out that he had been unable to find a case in which Ohio failed to recognize a marriage carried out in another state. "You have, under Due Process, the notion that once you are married, that attaches all kinds of vested rights," Gerhardstein argued. "You have important parenting rights. You have important child-rearing rights that have been recognized by the Supreme Court. For history, that has been transportable across state lines."[11]

Kentucky Attorney General Jack Conway had declined to appeal the original ruling in *Bourke v. Beshear*, and Governor Steve Beshear hired outside attorneys to try to overturn the ruling. The law firm of VanAntwerp, Monge, Jones, Edwards & McCann, LLP, was hired to handle the case. The lead attorney was Leigh Gross Latherow, a Kentucky native with nearly twenty years of experience in law. Latherow built her argument on the *Windsor* ruling. In her interpretation, that decision affirmed the rights of the states to pass laws against same-sex marriage while striking down any federal bans. The state's marriage statutes and its constitutional amendment defining marriage as being between a man and a woman did not change the law. Instead, they reflected the beliefs of the state's citizens and its marriage traditions.

Kentucky's argument also centered around procreation, and the state's belief that marriage functioned as providing a stable environment into which children can be born and raised. Latherow argued that the state's marriage laws and recognition of heterosexual marriages were directly linked to the state's interest in furthering procreation.

"Same-sex couples do not further that interest and, therefore, restricting the benefits and burdens of marriage do not violate the Fourteenth Amendment," Latherow argued. "The petitioners' contention that procreation would not be harmed if the state granted them a marriage license or recognized their out-of-state marriage license applies the wrong test."[12]

Laura Landenwich, the attorney for the respondents, argued that Kentucky's law "placed a badge of inferiority on people and families," and that it intruded on the individual rights guaranteed by the Constitution. The arguments that the state used to defend the ban—that it was up to the state to decide whether or not to allow same-sex marriage—were the same as those that were raised and rejected when other courts overturned marriage bans.

"The fundamental right to marry has not changed," Landenwich said during oral arguments. "What has changed is our understanding of what it means to be gay and lesbian. And now we must recognize that these individuals are entitled to the equal protection of the law, and they are entitled to exercise their fundamental right."[13]

Tennessee's arguments were similar to Kentucky's. Tennessee Associate Solicitor Joseph Whalen offered the argument that the state did not discriminate against same-sex couples by denying them marriage rights. In fact, Tennessee law forbade recognition of any marriage not recognized by the state, rather than singling out any one group. The state's marriage law was intended to provide a stable environment for children. "The Constitution does not demand Tennessee recognize same-sex marriage," Whalen said.[14]

The appellees' arguments, made by attorney Bill Harbison, centered on the belief that Tennessee's law violated the Fourteenth Amendment and deprived the parties of due protection under the law. Those same protections were, however, extended to other married couples. The Fourteenth Amendment prohibits Tennessee from disregarding existing marriages, Harbison argued:

> Tennessee's Non-Recognition Laws strip petitioners of both the status and the protections of marriage, stigmatize their families, deprive them of critical legal protections, and leave them vulnerable to harm in virtually every aspect of their lives. None of the interests that respondents have asserted can justify the intentional imposition of such profoundly unequal treatment.[15]

Ruling for the Appellees

After the oral arguments wrapped up on August 6, supporters of same-sex marriage and their opponents settled in to wait for the ruling. The nation as a whole had shifted its attitude regarding same-sex marriages in recent years, and other decisions striking down gay marriage bans had been upheld under appeal. Since the *Windsor* ruling struck down DOMA, there had been more than twenty cases brought to federal courts on behalf of same-sex couples seeking the right to marry. None of those cases had gone against same-sex marriage.

Weeks of waiting for a verdict turned into a month. The first month dragged into a second month before the judges issued their decision. On November 6, 2014, they announced their decision. In a ruling that they called *DeBoer v. Snyder*, the justices found in favor of the states. The vote was 2-1, with judges Sutton and Cook siding with the states and Daugherty voting for the couples. In the eyes of the Sixth Circuit Court of Appeals, the state laws did not violate the US Constitution.[16]

In the majority opinion written by Sutton, the court sided with the states on the question of whether it is in the power of voters and legislators to pass laws governing who can get married. The opinion also referred back to 1972's *Baker v. Nelson* decision by the US Supreme Court. The *Baker* ruling had not yet been overturned. Until that happened, there would be no legal grounds for that ruling to be ignored or considered redundant. Sutton's opinion also supported the states' more questionable claims that the marriage laws were in place as a way to support the growth of families.[17]

By creating a status (marriage) and by subsidizing it (e.g., with tax-filing privileges and deductions), the States created an incentive for two people who procreate together to stay together for purposes of rearing offspring. That does not convict the States of irrationality, only of awareness of the biological reality that couples of the same sex do not have children in the same way as couples of opposite sexes and that couples of the same sex do not run the risk of unintended offspring. That explanation, still relevant today, suffices to allow the States to retain authority over an issue they have regulated from the beginning.[18]

The majority opinion also pointed out the fact that the plaintiffs in the cases had limited their own definitions of marriage to two adults, whether gay, bisexual, or heterosexual. "If it is constitutionally irrational to stand by the man-woman definition of marriage, it must be constitutionally irrational to stand by the monogamous definition of marriage. Plaintiffs have no answer to the point."[19]

Judge Daugherty wrote a dissenting opinion, in which she sharply criticized the state laws in question and the ruling by her fellow judges. She likened the majority opinion to "an engrossing TED Talk or, possibly, an introductory lecture in Political Philosophy." In her view, the majority opinion also dodged answering the main question of whether bans on same-sex marriage violated the Fourteenth Amendment.[20]

She speculated that the goal of the majority ruling may have been to force the Supreme Court to take up the matter of same-sex marriage. Daugherty wrote,

Because the correct result is so obvious, one is tempted to speculate that the majority has purposefully taken the contrary position to create the circuit split regarding the legality of same-sex marriage that could prompt a grant of certiorari by the Supreme Court and an end to the uncertainty of status and the interstate chaos that the current discrepancy in state laws threatens.[21]

The ruling disappointed supporters of same-sex marriage, as well as the plaintiffs who saw the earlier rulings in their favor overturned. It also created the situation that Daugherty described. The Sixth Circuit Court of Appeals ruling clashed with earlier rulings by the Fourth, Seventh, Ninth, and Tenth Circuits, all of which had found state bans on same-sex marriage to be unconstitutional. The Sixth Circuit's finding that it was bound by *Baker v. Nelson* to uphold the bans created a split with those earlier court rulings. Supreme Court Justice Ruth Bader Ginsburg had even publicly stated that the Supreme Court had not taken up the issue because there had not been a split.[22]

Obergefell and the other plaintiffs had two options. They could ask the entire Sixth Circuit bench for what is called an en banc hearing. The appeals court ruling would be wiped out and the case would be heard by all of the judges of the appeals court, instead of a panel of three. The loser of the en banc hearing would be able to appeal to the Supreme Court. The Supreme Court would be unlikely to take the case until its next session after the en banc hearing, delaying the outcome.

Their other option was to appeal directly to the Supreme Court. If they filed an appeal soon after the ruling, their case might come before the Supreme Court before its term ended in the summer of 2015. Ultimately, the plaintiffs in *DeBoer v. Snyder*, *Obergefell v. Hodges*, *Bourke v. Beshear*, and *Tanco v. Haslam* decided to petition the Supreme Court to hear their case.

CHAPTER 5
A Case for the Plaintiff

On November 14, 2014, following the ruling by the Sixth Circuit Court of Appeals, lawyers for the *Obergefell v. Hodges* case filed a petition for writ of certiorari with the US Supreme Court. A certiorari petition is the document in which the losing party in a court case seeks review from the Supreme Court of the United States. In October, the Supreme Court had refused to grant the petitions filed in the aftermath of lower court rulings on same-sex marriage. Instead, the Court had let stand the decisions striking down bans on same-sex marriage, which cleared the way for five more states to begin issuing marriage licenses to same-sex couples.

Nonetheless, observers widely expected the Supreme Court to take up the matter of same-sex marriage soon and settle an issue that was becoming divisive and problematic across the country. When the Court had consented to hear *Hollingsworth v. Perry* in 2012, same-sex marriage was legal in nine states as well as Washington, DC. After the *Windsor* ruling of mid-2013,

The US Supreme Court building is in Washington, DC.

many judges used the decision as a precedent in ruling in favor of same-sex marriage.[1] By the time Obergefell appealed to the Supreme Court, thirty-six states had approved gay marriage.

Americans on both sides of the issue deemed it time for the Supreme Court to resolve the patchwork of laws concerning same-sex marriage that had arisen across the country. The nation had seen a fundamental cultural shift towards approval of gay marriage. 70 percent of Americans lived in states where same-sex marriage was legal. In 2001, 57 percent of Americans opposed gay marriage, while only 35 percent approved of it. Public opinion changed quickly, however, and in 2014, 52 percent supported gay marriage and 40 percent opposed it. Gay rights activists believed that they were on the cusp of civil rights triumph, in which same-sex couples across the nation would finally be granted the same rights and benefits of marriage as opposite-sex couples. By contrast, opponents of same-sex marriage hoped that the advances of same-sex marriage would be rolled back and the issue returned to individual states to legalize, limit, or prohibit.[2]

On January 16, 2015, the Supreme Court indicated that the moment had arrived. Previously, the Court had suggested that there was no pressing urgency in addressing the issue so long as lower court rulings were in accord with each other. With the Sixth Circuit Court upholding gay marriage bans, however, the rulings were split. The Supreme Court announced that it would hear the case of *Obergefell v. Hodges* in April.

Framing the Case

The Supreme Court is the highest court in the United States. Most of the cases argued before the Supreme Court are appeals of lower court decisions. Every year, the Court receives about 7,000 requests to review cases. It grants about 100 to 150 of these. The Court is made up of nine justices, and four of them must vote to hear a case. Law clerks help review petitions for certiorari. Each justice is assisted by three or four law clerks, who are recent graduates from law school.

Supreme Court justices are nominated by the president and must be confirmed by the Senate. At the time that *Obergefell v. Hodges* was heard, the Chief Justice of the United States was John Roberts, who was named in 2005 by President George W. Bush. The chief justice presides over public hearings and private conferences. If the chief justice votes with the majority opinion when ruling on a case, he has the power to decide who will write the opinion or to choose to write it himself. Otherwise, the justice with the most seniority will select who writes the opinion.

The eight associate justices ascended to the Court over a range of political eras. Two justices were nominated by President Reagan: Antonin Scalia in 1986 and Anthony M. Kennedy, who took his seat in 1988. President George H. W. Bush named Clarence Thomas to the Court in 1991. President Clinton named Ruth Bader Ginsburg in 1993 and Stephen G. Breyer in 1994. Samuel Anthony Alito, named by President George W. Bush, took his seat in 2006. President Obama named Sonia Sotomayor to the Court in 2009 and Elena Kagan in 2010.

Presidents tend to nominate justices whose views correspond with their own ideology. Nonetheless, candidates must be confirmed by the Senate, which would be unlikely to approve a judge with extremist tendencies. Therefore, presidents often pick candidates with such unimpeachable judicial credentials that the Senate can't justify refusing a confirmation. Still, even though judges are held with upholding the Constitution without regard to special interests, justices nominated by Republicans tend to lean conservative and justices named by Democrats tend to lean liberal in deciding cases.

These are the nine justices who were sitting on the Supreme Court at the time of the *Obergefell* hearing. Front row (L-R): Associate Justice Clarence Thomas, Associate Justice Antonin Scalia, Chief Justice John Roberts, Associate Justice Anthony M. Kennedy and Associate Justice Ruth Bader Ginsburg. Back row (L-R): Associate Justice Sonia Sotomayor, Associate Justice Stephen Breyer, Associate Justice Samuel Alito and Associate Justice Elena Kagan.

The Supreme Court set oral arguments to be held on April 28, 2015, and scheduled deadlines for each side to file briefs. The Court also consolidated the four cases from Ohio, Michigan, Kentucky, and Tennessee, and ordered the plaintiffs and defendants to focus arguments on two questions:

1) Does the Fourteenth Amendment require a state to license a marriage between two people of the same sex?

2) Does the Fourteenth Amendment require a state to recognize a marriage between two people of the same sex when their marriage was lawfully licensed and performed out-of-state?[3]

Oral arguments before the Supreme Court generally last an hour—a half hour per side—but *Obergefell v. Hodges* was allotted a total of two and a half hours.

On February 27, lawyers for the petitioners submitted their briefs, one for each of the four original cases. Each document stated the facts of the case and made an argument for their position supporting same-sex marriage. The petitioners were limited to presenting arguments on the issues relevant to their specific case. Therefore, *Obergefell v. Hodges* and *Tanco v. Haslam* addressed the second question, concerning recognition of out-of-state same-sex marriages. *DeBoer v. Snyder* addressed the first question, on requiring states to issue marriage licenses to same-sex couples, and *Bourke v. Beshear* addressed both. Lawyers for the respondents—Hodges and the governors of Michigan, Kentucky, and Tennessee—submitted briefs stating their side of the case on March 27. These were followed on April 17 by reply briefs from the petitioners, in which they countered the positions put forward by the respondents.[4]

Meanwhile, the Court received nearly 150 *amicus curiae* briefs, also called friend-of-the-court briefs. These are briefs containing arguments or recommendations that are filed by people or groups who are not directly involved in the case but have an interest in the outcome. Briefs were submitted by law professors, experts, and scholars. Various states submitted briefs, and US senators and House representatives also signed onto briefs. Mayors from cities across the county filed a brief supporting the petitioners, while national Republican leaders supported the respondents. Groups and individuals submitted briefs supporting one side or the other—the American Bar Association, the American Federation of Labor and Congress of Industrial Organizations, the American Psychological Association, and Human Rights Watch, for example, supported the petitioners, while many conservative organizations and a significant number of religious associations supported the respondents.[5]

On March 6, the United States submitted a friend-of-the-court brief supporting the petitioners. President Obama had announced his support of same-sex marriage in 2012. The brief argued that laws banning same-sex marriage discriminated against couples and children by denying them protections and benefits granted by opposite-sex marriage. It also pointed to the reasoning in *Windsor* as rationale for rejecting state bans of same-sex marriage. The government's brief was signed by US Solicitor General Donald B. Verrilli.[6]

Each petitioner had a formidable legal team working on the case. The Court, however, requested that a single lawyer present oral arguments on each issue. On March 31, lawyers for the petitioners announced their selections. Mary Bonauto would be allotted thirty minutes on the first question and Douglas Hallward-Driemeier would have thirty minutes to argue the second question. The petitioners requested that the counsel for the United States—US Solicitor General Donald B. Verrilli—have fifteen minutes to argue the first question, as well. The Court consented.[7]

Civil rights attorney Mary Bonauto, representing April DeBoer, was an experienced activist and trial lawyer credited with helping craft a long-term strategy for same-sex marriage to gain public support and win legalization in the states. Since 1990, Bonauto had worked on civil rights issues for GLAD (GLBTQ Legal Advocates and Defenders). She represented plaintiffs in the 1999 case of *Baker v. Vermont*, which argued that same-sex couples were legally entitled to the rights and benefits of marriage. The case led to Vermont becoming the first state to establish civil unions, in 2000. Bonauto used the same arguments in the landmark 2003 case of *Goodridge v. Department of Public Health*, which resulted in Massachusetts becoming the first state to legalize same-sex marriage in 2004. (Bonauto herself married her long-term partner, Jennifer Wriggins, in Massachusetts in 2008.) She achieved the first federal court victories against DOMA in the case *Gill v. Office of Personnel Management*, filed in 2009. *Gill* laid the groundwork for the eventual Supreme Court ruling in *Windsor*. In 2014, Bonauto was named a MacArthur Fellow, recognized with what is sometimes called a "genius grant."[8]

Douglas Hallward-Driemeier joined the Tennessee plaintiffs' case in 2014, following the ruling by the Sixth Circuit Court of Appeals. A former Rhodes Scholar, which had allowed him to study at the University of Oxford, Hallward-Driemeier had

Mary Bonauto is known for her work in cases related to civil rights, including the rights of the LGBT community.

worked on cases for the US Department of Justice for eleven years before returning to private practice. He had argued before the Supreme Court in fifteen previous cases. Hallward-Driemeier was familiar with LGBT legal issues, as well. He had helped draft *amicus curiae* briefs in cases involving LGBT rights, including one on behalf of the Anti-Defamation League in *Windsor*.[9]

Donald B. Verrilli had served as solicitor general since 2011. Before that, he held the position of deputy counsel to President Obama and as an associate deputy attorney general in the Department of Justice. The role of the solicitor general is to represent the US government before the Supreme Court. The solicitor general chooses which cases to seek to bring before the Court and determines the government's position. Verrilli had participated in dozens of oral arguments before the Supreme Court, including *Windsor*, in which he held that Section 3 of DOMA violated equal protection.[10]

Due Process

The concept of due process is a venerable tradition dating back to 1215, when the English charter, the Magna Carta, granted certain rights and liberties under the law. Due process in the American Constitution is described in the Fifth Amendment, which stated that no person shall "be deprived of life, liberty, or property, without due process of law."[11]

There are two aspects to due process: procedural and substantive. Procedural due process guarantees the right to fair treatment under the law concerning procedures such as trials. Substantive due process requires that the law respect certain fundamental liberties. Therefore, due process protects the freedom to marry as a fundamental right. Many advocates of same-sex marriage used this argument in court cases.

The Fifth Amendment requires that the federal government respect due process of American citizens. The Fourteenth Amendment extends the provisions in the Bill of Rights—which includes the Fifth Amendment—to state and local governments.

One landmark case involving substantive due process was *Meyer v. State of Nebraska* (1923), which struck down a state law prohibiting the teaching of foreign languages. The opinion gave a broad description of the rights protected by due process:

> Without doubt, it denotes not merely freedom from bodily restraint, but also the right of the individual to contract, to engage in any of the common occupations of life, to acquire useful knowledge, to marry, establish a home and bring up children, to worship God according to the dictates of his own conscience, and generally to enjoy those privileges long recognized at common law as essential to the orderly pursuit of happiness by free men.[12]

The Argument

April 28 was a beautiful, sunny day, and a large crowd had gathered outside the Supreme Court. Most of the people rallying were supporters of same-sex marriage who were jubilantly anticipating a victory. Protesters were also in attendance. People had been waiting in line for days hoping for a seat inside to watch the oral arguments.[13]

The oral arguments before the Supreme Court provide the moment of greatest public exposure for a case under consideration. The justices, however, aren't primarily interested in hearing a summary of the briefs. Oral arguments give them an opportunity to ask questions based on the facts and positions put forward in the briefs. Every member of the Court except for Justice Thomas had questions or comments during the arguments. Overall, justices thought to lean toward opposing same-sex marriage asked more questions of the petitioners, while justices believed to be more supportive had more questions for the respondents.

Proceedings began at 10 a.m. with Chief Justice Roberts announcing that the Court would be hearing arguments on the consolidated cases. Bonauto opened by arguing that the same-sex couples were constitutionally entitled to the "legal commitment, responsibility and protection that is marriage." After a short statement, the first question arose, with Justice Ginsburg asking about the states' role in domestic relations with consideration to *Windsor*.[14]

Some of the most critical issues were introduced early on during the interchanges between Bonauto and the justices. As Ginsburg indicated, the *Windsor* ruling had recognized that the states traditionally held authority over the laws regulating marriage. Bonauto replied that regardless, state laws must respect people's constitutional rights, which were being denied in banning same-sex marriage.[15]

Chief Justice Roberts immediately brought up the matter of the core definition of marriage. One of the petitioners' key contentions was that they were not trying to claim same-sex marriage as a new constitutional right. Rather, they were trying to gain equal access to a fundamental right—the institution of marriage—that was being denied them. Roberts asserted, "You're not seeking to join the institution, you're seeking to change what the institution is." Bonauto replied that the

Fourteenth Amendment provided "enduring guarantees" of equality even when society's views changed over time.[16]

Justice Kennedy then expressed skepticism over the fast pace of these changes. "This definition has been with us for millennia. And it—it's very difficult for the Court to say, oh, well, we—we know better." Bonauto responded with examples of how marriage had indeed changed with time, such as by granting more rights to women and ending bans on interracial marriage. She also stressed circumstances specific to the United States: "When it affirmed the Fourteenth Amendment in 1868, that's when we made—our nation collectively made a commitment to individual liberty and equality."[17]

Roberts also questioned whether legalizing same-sex marriage would prematurely close public debate on the issue. "People feel very differently about something if they have a chance to vote on it than if it's imposed on them by—by the courts." Bonauto replied by pointing out the ongoing hardships imposed on couples and families by slow change, such as by the Michigan couple who could not both legally adopt their children. Earlier, she had pointed out that "waiting is not neutral."[18]

Some questions explored the possible consequences of legalizing same-sex marriage. Justice Alito questioned whether, as a result, a group of two men and two women could legally be granted a marriage license. Bonauto answered that no, such a case would involve many other legal issues. Justices also expressed concerns about clergy being forced to perform same-sex marriages despite religious objections. Bonauto replied that the First Amendment protected against the possibility.

Justice Kagan jumped in to mention the analogy that rabbis could refuse to marry Jews and non-Jews.[19]

At this point, a protester in the audience interrupted proceedings, screaming out, "Homosexuality is an abomination!" After he was removed by security, it was time for US Solicitor General Verrilli to present his arguments.[20]

Verrilli began by making several points regarding states denying "the equal dignity of their relationships" for same-sex couples in states that banned same-sex marriage. If the Court declined to uphold same-sex marriage, it would be validating the second-class status of these couples. Conceivably, the long-term outcome could be an ingrained two-tier system of some states that recognized and others that denied the validity of same-sex marriage. This would result in significant "costs of constitutional stature."[21]

Verrilli concentrated on addressing same-sex marriage in terms of equal protection. Same-sex couples deserved to be treated as equals in the community under the law. Denying the protections of marriage impacted couples and their families:

[Y]ou have hundreds of thousands of children raised in same-sex households now. And what Respondents' position and Respondents' caution argument leads you to is the conclusion that those hundreds of thousands of children don't get the stabilizing structure and the many benefits of marriage.[22]

Next, John J. Bursch argued for the respondents for forty-five minutes. Bonauto was then allotted a few minutes for a rebuttal.

After a short break, Douglas Hallward-Driemeier argued the second question for the petitioners regarding the recognition of out-of-state same-sex marriages. This portion of the argument would be relevant to the final decision only if the Court ruled for the respondents on the first question about issuing marriage licenses to same-sex couples.

Hallward-Driemeier began by stating that a refusal to recognize out-of-state same-sex marriages allowed a state to "effectively dissolve that marriage without a sufficiently important justification to do so." In response to a question by Justice Scalia, he clarified that a state should be required to recognize a marriage even when it wasn't lawful under that state's law. The justices brought up other examples in which marriages in one state might be illegal in others—such as polygamy, underage marriage, and marriage of cousins. Hallward-Driemeier stated that a state should have a "sufficiently important interest" in order to deny recognition of an out-of-state marriage. A refusal to recognize out-of-state same-sex marriages was a "stark departure from the State's traditional practice of recognizing out-of-state marriages even though they could not have been celebrated within the State."[23]

Chief Justice Roberts suggested that if even a single state permitted same-sex marriage, and all others were required to recognize out-of-state same-sex marriages, that one state could essentially set the policy for the entire nation. Later in his argument, Hallward-Driemeier contended that when one state allows same-sex couples to establish relationships and families under the protection of the law, other states should not be allowed to destroy those marriages through legal pretexts.[24]

The subject of same-sex marriage is hotly debated. Here people who are against same-sex marriages protest outside the Supreme Court.

CHAPTER 6
The Defense Argues

The respondents in *Obergefell v. Hodges* were tasked with defending state bans on same-sex marriage and justifying a refusal to recognize out-of-state same-sex marriages. As with the petitioners, the lawyers for each of the four consolidated cases considered only the question pertinent to their specific case. On March 27, 2015, they submitted briefs arguing their positions.

The respondents consistently denied that the Fourteenth Amendment could be interpreted to require same-sex marriage or the recognition of out-of-state same-sex marriages. The brief for the *DeBoer v. Snyder* case stated, for example, that the Amendment said "nothing about how to define marriage or the policy goals marriage must serve."[1]

Many of the arguments also linked the issue to state sovereignty and the threat of federalism encroaching on states' democratic processes. Who had the right to decide issues related to same-sex marriage state legislatures and voters of each state or the courts? The respondents overwhelmingly considered the power reserved for the states. Several of the briefs outlined the history of marriage in their state and expressed indignation at the prospect of the federal government encroaching on their perceived authority in the area of domestic relations. As stated in the Ohio brief, "Our Constitution establishes local debate and consensus as the usual method for social change." In this view, the entire country benefited from states having the freedom to adopt different approaches to the issue of same-sex marriage.[2]

The respondents also defended the rationale behind their laws concerning same-sex marriage. Opposite-sex marriage was portrayed as traditional and the notion of same-sex marriage an attempt to redefine the institution. Same-sex couples did not have any fundamental right to marry, in this view. If a state never in its history recognized the marriages of same-sex couples, it was merely applying its own rule of law in refusing to recognize out-of-state same-sex marriages.[3]

The briefs also addressed petitioners' claims that their constitutional rights of equal protection were being violated by the state's laws. There are various ways that judges test whether a law is discriminatory. The most lenient level is the "rational basis" test. This review seeks to determine whether a law serves a legitimate government interest. In some cases, laws are required to meet "heightened scrutiny," or the more demanding "strict scrutiny" test. These require that the law be shown to fulfill a compelling government interest. If a law doesn't pass a rational basis review or stricter test, it can be argued that it is motivated by prejudice, disapproval, private biases, or hostility to a group. Previous to the ruling by the Sixth Circuit Court of Appeals, many judges had rejected laws banning same-sex marriage using one of these tests.[4]

It was widely assumed that the Supreme Court would use the rational basis test in determining whether the states' laws on same-sex marriage were constitutional. Each one of the briefs devoted space to defending the rational basis behind the "traditional" definition of marriage or explaining how the laws promoted state interests. They also argued that heightened scrutiny was not warranted in their cases.

The briefs put forth a variety of justifications intended to demonstrate that their laws served legitimate purposes. These included many arguments made in previous cases, such as the procreative purpose of marriage, promotion of birth rates, and the different contributions brought by opposite-sex parents.

Justifying the Marriage Bans

The respondents chose John J. Bursch, special assistant attorney general of Michigan, to argue before the Court in defense of state bans on same-sex marriage. A lawyer in private practice and former solicitor general of the state from 2011 to 2013, he had appeared before the Supreme Court nine times previously. His highest profile case was *Schuette v. Coalition to Defend Affirmative Action* in 2013, in which the Court upheld a voter-approved constitutional amendment prohibiting the use of race-based preferences in state university admissions.

Bursch's law firm, however, declined to represent the state of Michigan in same-sex marriage case, declaring it too controversial. Bursch took leave from his employer in order to concentrate on *Obergefell v. Hodges.*[5]

Because the petitioners had chosen to divide their time on the first question between Bonauto and Verrilli, Bursch's slot of forty-five minutes was the longest appearance of any attorney before the Court during the arguments. He opened by stating his position:

> This case isn't about how to define marriage. It's about who gets to decide that question. Is it the people acting through the democratic process, or is it the Federal courts? And we're asking you to affirm every individual's fundamental liberty interest in deciding the meaning of marriage.[6]

Justice Breyer almost immediately brought up the issue of the exclusion of same-sex couples from marriage:

> Marriage, as the States administer it, is open to vast numbers of people who both have children, adopt children, don't have children, all over the place. But there is one group of people whom they won't open marriage to. So they have no possibility to participate in that fundamental liberty. That is people of the same sex who wish to marry. And so we ask, why? And the answer we get is, well, people have always done it. You know, you could have answered that one the same way we talk about racial segregation.[7]

A dominant issue was the matter of whether extending marriage to same-sex couples would harm the institution. Bursch contended that "when you change the definition of marriage to delink the idea that we're binding children with their biological mom and dad, that has consequences." Later on, he stated, "[T]he State doesn't have an interest in love and emotion at all." The justices expressed skepticism. Justice Sotomayor wondered, "How does withholding marriage from one group, same-sex couples, increase the value to the other group?" Justice Kennedy rejected "some premise that only opposite-sex couples can have a bonding with the child." Justice Kagan asked whether, if the purpose of marriage was solely procreation, marriage licenses could be denied to any couple that did not plan to have children. Justice Ginsburg asked about the hypothetical case of a seventy-year-old couple.[8]

Chief Justice Roberts brought up an alternate perspective on the situation: "I mean, if Sue loves Joe and Tom loves Joe, Sue can marry him and Tom can't. And the difference is based upon their different sex. Why isn't that a straightforward question of sexual discrimination?" Regardless of the validity of the sex discrimination argument, it did not end up being pertinent to the final ruling.[9]

At one point, Bursch referenced the rising out-of-wedlock birthrate since 1970. Justice Sotomayor responded that it wasn't related to the recent legalization in same-sex marriages, and Kennedy pointed out, "[U]nder your view, it would be very difficult for same-sex couples to adopt some of these children."[10]

After Bursch finished his arguments, Bonauto had a few minutes for rebuttal. She contended that extending marriage to same-sex couples would not change the institution. She also rebuffed the idea that allowing same-sex marriage would affect opposite-sex couples' decisions on having children.

Arguing Against Marriage Recognition

Tennessee Associate Solicitor General Joseph Whalen argued the second question for the respondents. Whalen had never before appeared before the Supreme Court, but he had worked for the state of Tennessee since 1999 and had extensive experience filing briefs and making arguments in state appellate courts. His previous highest-profile case was the 2002 lawsuit of death row inmate Abu-Ali Abdur'Rahman, in which he served as second-chair attorney to the state attorney general before the Supreme Court. The state won the case.[11]

Whalen had thirty minutes to argue his case opposing recognition of out-of-state same-sex marriages. He defended the position:

> [S]o long as we're talking about a marriage from another State that is not the man-woman definition, that it is simply the State's interest in maintaining a cohesive and a coherent internal State policy with regard to marriage that justifies not recognizing those marriages.[12]

At one point, Chief Justice Roberts asked, "Outside of the present controversy, when was the last time Tennessee declined to recognize a marriage from out of state?" Whalen replied that that the last instance was 1970, regarding a father and stepdaughter, and acknowledged that it was rare to refuse to recognize an out-of-state marriage. Whalen ended with a discussion of federalism and a plea to accommodate different viewpoints among states on same-sex marriage.

In a brief rebuttal, Hallward-Driemeier reiterated some of the real-life consequences of Tennessee's law. He talked about how non-recognition laws could lead to one member of a same-sex couple being treated as "a legal stranger with no right to visit her child" when their daughter is hospitalized. He urged the court once again to reject the "second-class status" of same-sex marriages.

Questioning Judges

After the oral arguments were concluded, the public window into the case was closed until the ruling, which was expected in late June. As a matter of procedure, the members of the Court vote on how to decide a case later in the week in a Justices' Conference. They often discuss the details of cases beforehand with law clerks, but only the justices attend the Conference. Each justice, beginning with the chief justice, is given time to offer opinions and concerns about the case. They then cast votes in the same order. The chief justice or the senior justice in the majority assigns which justice will write the majority opinion of the Court, and the same process determines who will write the dissent. Any justice voting with the majority can write a concurring opinion that may present different arguments for the ruling, and any justice can write a separate dissent.

Meanwhile, observers and pundits on both sides of the same-sex marriage issue analyzed the text of the April 28 oral arguments in an attempt to predict the Court's ruling. The questions and comments of the four liberal-leaning justices—Ginsburg, Breyer, Sotomayor, and Kagan—seemed to indicate that they would support same-sex marriage, although Breyer betrayed reservations about the Court moving quickly to decide an issue that was still in flux among the states. The four conservative-leaning justices—Roberts, Scalia, Thomas, and Alito—gave little indication of abandoning their opposition.

The closest-watched justice, however, was Kennedy, the so-called "swing vote." Both sides found reason to hope that he was inclined toward their view. He expressed trepidation about the Court intervening to leave a mark on an institution that had existed for millennia, but he also appeared unconvinced by the procreation-centered view of marriage portrayed by the respondents.

Anthony Kennedy: The Swing Vote

Anthony Kennedy was nominated to the Supreme Court by President Ronald Reagan, a fellow Californian, and confirmed in the Senate in 1988 by a vote of 97-0. As is typical of nominees, he avoided mentioning specific positions on issues during confirmation hearings. While serving as judge on the Ninth Circuit Court of Appeals from 1975 onward, Kennedy had established a reputation as a judge with integrity who ruled on a case-by-case basis rather than adhering to an ideological agenda.

Anthony Kennedy was nominated by President Ronald Reagan to become a Supreme Court justice. He took his seat in 1988.

His tenure on the Supreme Court confirmed this reputation. Kennedy came to be considered a "swing vote" who sided with liberal justices on some cases and with the conservatives on others. He has, however, established himself as a strong proponent of individual liberties. He authored landmark opinions supporting gay rights and marriage equality in 1996, 2003, and 2013. Nonetheless, in the days leading up to the announcement of the *Obergefell* ruling, observers did not take his vote for granted. His questions and comments during oral arguments seemed to indicate doubts about the merits of both viewpoints. Ultimately, though, his role in guaranteeing same-sex couples the right to marry is likely to stand as one of his most enduring legacies.

The Dignity of Marriage

One dominant theme among both sides of the issue was the matter of dignity in marriage. This emphasis was undoubtedly intended with Kennedy's consideration in mind. In supporting same-sex marriage in past rulings, he had often referred to the "dignity" of the institution. In *Windsor*, he had described same-sex marriage as "a relationship deemed by the State worthy of dignity in the community equal with all other marriages." Therefore, Bonauto opened her remarks with a mention of "the basic constitutional commitment to equal dignity." Verrilli began by stating, "The opportunity to marry is integral to human dignity." Bursch quickly assured the Court that "the marriage institution did not develop to deny dignity or to give second class status to anyone." Hallward-Driemeier stated of Obergefell and his husband that "the State has no legitimate interest for denying them the dignity," by including the fact of their marriage on the death certificate.

Kennedy himself brought up the matter of dignity multiple times during the oral arguments. He pointed out, "Same-sex couples say, of course, we understand the nobility and the sacredness of the marriage. We know we can't procreate, but we want the other attributes of it in order to show that we, too, have a dignity that can be fulfilled." Observers were left wondering if, along with other factors such as federalism, equal protection, due process, and the definition of the institution, dignity could prove relevant in the upcoming ruling.[13]

CHAPTER 7

The Justices Decide

T he ruling in *Obergefell v. Hodges* came at the conclusion of the Supreme Court's 2015 session. As the petitioners had hoped, their cases would be settled by the end of the session. Previous court rulings had overturned (or, in the case of the Sixth Circuit, upheld) bans on same-sex marriage in individual states. By the time the case made it to the Court, the number of states still banning same-sex marriage had shrunk to only fourteen.

The stakes were high for supporters of same-sex marriage. If the justices decided same-sex marriage bans violated the Constitution, every state would be required to treat every married couple equally, regardless of sexual orientation. In the event that the Court upheld the bans, the decision could mean reversals in other states and could put married same-sex couples in a state of legal limbo. If that happened, no one knew whether same-sex marriages would still be recognized, or whether lesbian and gay couples could still get married in states where bans had previously been overturned.

Obergefell (right) leaves the Supreme Court building with Chad Griffin, the president of the Human Rights Campaign. This photo was taken on June 22, just days before the justices announced their decision.

Overturning Bans

Skies over Washington, DC, were overcast on June 26, 2015, the day that the Supreme Court issued its verdict in *Obergefell v. Hodges*. Nearly two months had passed since the conclusion of oral arguments, and both sides of the case were on edge, waiting for the verdict. Jim Obergefell had returned to the Court repeatedly in June, unsure of when the decision might be announced. Other plaintiffs and supporters also traveled back and forth or stayed close to the Court.

The weather may have appeared ominous, but the day proved to be a happy one for Obergefell and his fellow plaintiffs. By a 5-4 margin, the Court ruled that the Fourteenth Amendment requires all states to allow same-sex marriages.

Same-sex marriage would now be legal in all fifty states, Washington, DC, and the US territories.[1]

The decision also struck down the Supreme Court's only other ruling on same-sex marriage—the 1972 *Baker v. Nelson* decision. The majority opinion acknowledged that the debate over same-sex marriage and whether gay and lesbian couples have a right to wed would continue, and that opponents would continue to voice their point of view. It also affirmed that people who oppose same-sex marriage would have the right to express their opinions under the freedom of speech protections within the First Amendment.[2]

Finding for the Plaintiff

Justices Breyer, Ginsburg, Kagan, Kennedy, and Sotomayor made up the majority who favored same-sex marriage. The majority opinion was written by Kennedy, who many had predicted would serve as the crucial swing vote and who had written the majority opinion in the *Windsor* decision.[3]

In his twenty-eight-page opinion, Kennedy made it clear that the Court's ruling was expanding the existing fundamental right to marry to lesbian and gay couples, rather than granting a new right, and that these couples had a right to the dignity bestowed by marriage. The Court's ruling also granted protections to same-sex couples who were already married. Many of those couples had gotten married following earlier court rulings that had overturned state bans. In some places, legal recognition of their marriages had been put on hold until the Supreme Court could rule in *Obergefell v. Hodges*.[4]

The majority opinion was solidly rooted in the Fourteenth Amendment, with both the Equal Protection Clause and the Due Process Clause factoring into the decision. By tying the ruling to the Constitution, the five justices in the majority made it impossible to undo the ruling without a formal amendment to the Constitution or a reversal in a future Supreme Court case.[5]

Kennedy opened his opinion with a description of the institution of marriage as one that had a place in both the secular and the religious world. He also reflected on how marriage has evolved over time, from the days when it was common for weddings to be arranged between families to a personal commitment between two people who love each other. Similarly, attitudes toward being gay had also shifted significantly since the days when homosexuality was viewed as an illness.[6]

The Supreme Court had long upheld marriage as a fundamental right, but in the past that right had been extended only to heterosexual couples. Kennedy stated that the protections and rights offered by marriage should apply equally to same-sex couples, and that they should have the right to celebrate their commitment to each other with dignity. He reasoned that marriage represents a unique way in which two people can demonstrate their commitment to each other, and the ability to decide whether or not to get married is an important right, regardless of the gender of one's chosen spouse. The Court also had a history of protecting the right to marry because of the protections that marriage grants to families. Same-sex couples have the same right to form a family, Kennedy wrote:

In forming a marital union, two people become something greater than once they were. As some of the petitioners in these cases demonstrate, marriage embodies a love that may endure even past death. It would misunderstand these men and women to say they disrespect the idea of marriage. Their plea is that they do respect it, respect it so deeply that they seek to find its fulfillment for themselves. Their hope is not to be condemned to live in loneliness, excluded from one of civilization's oldest institutions. They ask for equal dignity in the eyes of the law. The Constitution grants them that right.[7]

Kennedy rejected the arguments that same-sex marriage cheapened or devalued marriage for heterosexual couples. As in previous cases, he stressed the petitioners' desire to form a bond within the institution of marriage, noting:

[I]t is the enduring importance of marriage that underlies the petitioners' contentions. This, they say, is their whole point. Far from seeking to devalue marriage, the petitioners seek it for themselves because of their respect—and need—for its privileges and responsibilities.[8]

He went on to reference the *Lawrence* ruling of 2003, in which the Court struck down state laws that made sexual activity between two people of the same gender illegal. While that ruling gave gay and lesbian people a degree of freedom that had been unknown in some places, progress did not have to stop there. "Outlaw to outcast may be a step forward, but it does not achieve the full promise of liberty," Kennedy wrote.[9]

Kennedy cited several other prominent Supreme Court decisions that had reflected changing views and attitudes regarding the meaning of marriage. These included *Loving v. Virginia*, a 1967 case that struck down state laws against interracial marriage, as an example of how marriage should be a matter of personal choice. He also referenced the Court's 1965 ruling in *Griswold v. Connecticut*, which affirmed the right for married couples to use birth control and therefore a right to privacy upon which states could not intrude. The opinion also affirmed the right of churches and religious organizations that oppose same-sex marriage to do so under the protection of the First Amendment.[10]

Loving v. Virginia (1967)

In 1958, Virginia residents Mildred Jeter and Richard Loving were married in Washington, DC. Jeter was African American and Loving was white. When they returned to live in Virginia, they were arrested for violating the state's ban on marriage between interracial couples. They were sentenced to a year in jail with the sentence suspended if they left the state for twenty-five years.

The Lovings moved to Washington, DC, but in 1963, they filed a suit that reached the Supreme Court of Appeals of Virginia in 1965. The Court affirmed their convictions and upheld the state's anti-miscegenation

Mildred Jeter and Richard Loving's case regarding the lawfulness of interracial marriage at the Supreme Court was used as a precedent for same-sex marriages.

("mixing of racial groups") laws. At the time, sixteen states had laws against interracial marriage.

The Supreme Court heard the case in 1967. The justices unanimously struck down the law, citing the Equal Protection Clause and the Due Process Clause of the Fourteenth Amendment.

Same-sex marriage advocates held up the *Loving* ruling as a precedent in their arguments, and several court rulings referenced the case. In 2007, Mildred Loving herself voiced her support of the freedom to marry for all, including same-sex couples.[11]

Dissenting Opinions

The Court's four more conservative justices—Roberts, Thomas, Scalia, and Alito—all dissented from the ruling, as many court watchers had expected. Unusually, each of the four wrote a dissenting opinion to describe why he didn't vote in favor of Obergefell and the other plaintiffs.[12]

Chief Justice Roberts' dissent focused on the constitutional basis for overturning the state bans on same-sex marriage. He argued that allowing same-sex marriage might be a good and fair action to take, but that the Court should not play a role because marriage is not defined or discussed in the Constitution. He pointed out that in the previous six years, eleven states and Washington, DC, had changed their laws to allow same-sex marriage. "But this Court is not a legislature," he continued. "Whether same-sex marriage is a good idea should be of no concern to us. Under the Constitution, judges have the power to say what the law is, not what it should be."[13]

Roberts' dissent described the decision as "an act of will, not legal judgment," and criticized the five justices who made up the majority for wanting to "remake society." He also accused Kennedy and the others who voted in favor of same-sex marriage of reading the Fourteenth Amendment too broadly and of taking the power of legislating out of the hands of voters in those states that banned same-sex marriages. He concluded by urging supporters of same-sex marriage to celebrate the outcome, but not the legal reasoning behind it:

> If you are among the many Americans—of whatever sexual orientation—who favor expanding same-sex marriage, by all means celebrate today's decision. Celebrate the achievement of a desired goal. Celebrate the opportunity for a new expression of commitment to a partner. Celebrate the availability of new benefits. But do not celebrate the Constitution. It had nothing to do with it.[14]

Scalia's dissent echoed Roberts' argument that the Supreme Court was taking on the lawmaking powers of Congress. Known for his sharply-worded dissents, Scalia pulled no punches in criticizing the majority ruling. He agreed with Roberts' dissent in full, and went further by saying that the *Obergefell* decision lacked "even a thin veneer of law" and imposed the will of the Court on states in which voters and legislators had passed their own marriage laws. He described the substance of the ruling as not being of any great personal importance to himself, but objected to the manner in which the decision was reached and the personal sentiments involved in the majority opinion.[15]

"Buried beneath the mummeries and straining-to-be-memorable passages of the opinion is a candid and startling assertion," Scalia wrote. "No matter what it was the People ratified, the Fourteenth Amendment protects those rights

San Francisco holds an annual gay pride parade. In 2015, Obergefell had a place of honor in the parade after the monumental decision to legalize same-sex marriages.

that the Judiciary, in its 'reasoned judgment,' thinks the Fourteenth Amendment ought to protect." He noted that when the Fourteenth Amendment was ratified in 1868, every state in the union at that time defined marriage as between a man and a woman.[16]

He also criticized the Court for presuming to make the law, stating,

> [T]o allow the policy question of same-sex marriage to be considered and resolved by a select, patrician, highly unrepresentative panel of nine is to violate a principle even more fundamental than no taxation without representation: no social transformation without representation.[17]

Thomas's dissent made the argument that the Due Process clauses found in the Fifth and Fourteenth Amendments to the Constitution do not give the government the power to grant benefits to people. "In the American legal tradition, liberty has long been understood as individual freedom from governmental action, not as a right to a particular governmental entitlement," he wrote. According to him, the majority opinion undermined the political process and threatened religious liberty.[18]

Thomas also argued that the petitioners had not been deprived of liberty at all, at least not in the broad definition. "They have been able to travel freely around the country, making their homes where they please. Far from being incarcerated or physically restrained, petitioners have been left alone to order their lives as they see fit."[19]

Justice Alito's dissent centered around the argument that same-sex marriage is contrary to tradition. He cited the case *Washington v. Glucksberg* (1997), in which the Court ruled that the right to assisted suicide is not protected by the Due Process Clause. That ruling stated that the clause protected only rights that were deeply rooted in tradition, a circumstance that Alito argued did not apply to same-sex marriage. "For today's majority, it does not matter that the right to same-sex marriage lacks deep roots or even that it is contrary to long-established tradition," he wrote. "The justices in the majority claim the authority to confer constitutional protection upon that right simply because they believe that it is fundamental."[20]

In the Aftermath

With the *Obergefell v. Hodges* verdict, the United States joined twenty other countries in allowing same-sex couples to marry. Parades and victory rallies were held in cities across the country after the verdict was announced. Numerous celebrities and public figures spoke in support of the ruling, including candidates running to be the Democratic Party's nominee in the 2016 presidential election. Some large corporations temporarily changed their logos to display variations on the rainbow flag often used to express LGBT pride. Even the exterior of the White House was lit up in rainbow colors.[21]

President Barack Obama, who had publicly supported marriage equality since 2012, praised the ruling. "This ruling is a victory for America," Obama said in a speech at the White House. "This decision affirms what millions of Americans already believe in their hearts. When all Americans are truly treated as equal, we are more free."[22]

Opponents of same-sex marriage condemned the ruling as an overreach on the part of the Supreme Court. Just as Democratic Party presidential candidates spoke in favor of the ruling, the candidates for the Republican Party's nomination were quick to criticize the decision to varying degrees. They included Ohio Governor John Kasich, who was once linked to Obergefell's case. Kasich himself said that, if elected president, he would abide by the Court's ruling in the case.

Some conservative and religious groups even called for boycotts against companies that expressed support for the ruling. A legal backlash against the ruling also began. In the

The White House acknowledged the landmark decision in the *Obergefell* case by lighting up the front of the White House with rainbow-colored lights.

months following the ruling, several counties in Alabama, Kentucky, and Texas refused to issues marriage licenses to same-sex couples. Laws that discriminate against LGBT people in other ways have also been passed in some states, including a North Carolina law that stripped cities and towns of the power to pass their own anti-discrimination laws.

As Justice Kennedy wrote in the majority opinion, the debate over same-sex marriage will likely continue even as society gradually grows more accepting of gay and lesbian people. Attitudes toward gay, lesbian, and transgender people have evolved greatly in recent years and will likely continue to evolve. Jim Obergefell, who had worked for two years to have his marriage recognized and endured the death of his husband during that struggle, spoke eloquently about his hope for the future of marriage. "Today's ruling from the Supreme Court affirms what millions across the country already know to be true in our hearts: that our love is equal," he said. "It is my hope that the term gay marriage will soon be a thing of the past, that from this day forward it will be, simply, marriage."[23]

Questions to Consider

1. Should voters have a say in who can get married in their state?

2. How hard is it to amend the Constitution?

3. Why have attitudes toward same-sex marriage changed so much in such a short time?

4. What are some arguments in favor of same-sex marriage?

5. What are some arguments against same-sex marriage?

6. In what ways have gay and lesbian people been discriminated against?

7. Why are the protections granted under the Fourteenth Amendment important?

8. In what other cases has the Supreme Court struck down discriminatory laws?

9. Is discrimination against gay and lesbian people still a problem?

10. How can same-sex couples benefit from being married?

Primary Source Documents

Obergefell v. Hodges: Excerpts from the majority ruling, written by Justice Anthony Kennedy

I

The Constitution promises liberty to all within its reach, a liberty that includes certain specific rights that allow persons, within a lawful realm, to define and express their identity. The petitioners in these cases seek to find that liberty by marrying someone of the same sex and having their marriages deemed lawful on the same terms and conditions as marriages between persons of the opposite sex.

These cases come from Michigan, Kentucky, Ohio, and Tennessee, States that define marriage as a union between one man and one woman. The petitioners are 14 same-sex couples and two men whose same-sex partners are deceased. The respondents are state officials responsible for enforcing the laws in question. The petitioners claim the respondents violate the Fourteenth Amendment by denying them the right to marry or to have their marriages, lawfully performed in another State, given full recognition.

Petitioners filed these suits in United States District Courts in their home States. Each District Court ruled in their favor. Citations to those cases are in Appendix A, infra. The respondents appealed the decisions against them to the United States Court of Appeals for the Sixth Circuit. It consolidated the cases and reversed the judgments of the District Courts. The Court of Appeals held that a State has no constitutional obligation to license same-sex marriages or to recognize same-sex marriages performed out of State.

The petitioners sought certiorari. This Court granted review, limited to two questions. The first, presented by the cases from Michigan and Kentucky, is whether the Fourteenth Amendment requires a State to license a marriage between two people of the same sex. The second, presented by the cases from Ohio, Tennessee, and, again, Kentucky, is whether the Fourteenth Amendment requires a State to recognize a same-sex marriage licensed and performed in a State which does grant that right.

II

Before addressing the principles and precedents that govern these cases, it is appropriate to note the history of the subject now before the Court.

A

From their beginning to their most recent page, the annals of human history reveal the transcendent importance of marriage. The lifelong union of a man and a woman always has promised nobility and dignity to all persons, without regard to their station in life. Marriage is sacred to those who live by their religions and offers unique fulfillment to those who find meaning in the secular realm. Its dynamic allows two people to find a life that could not be found alone, for a marriage becomes greater than just the two persons.

Rising from the most basic human needs, marriage is essential to our most profound hopes and aspirations.

The centrality of marriage to the human condition makes it unsurprising that the institution has existed for millennia and across civilizations. Since the dawn of history, marriage has transformed strangers into relatives, binding families and societies together. Confucius taught that marriage lies at the foundation of government. This wisdom was echoed centuries later and half a world away by Cicero, who wrote, "The first bond of society is marriage; next, children; and then the family." There are untold references to the beauty of marriage in religious and philosophical texts spanning time, cultures, and faiths, as well as in art and literature in all their forms. It is fair and necessary to say these references were based on the understanding that marriage is a union between two persons of the opposite sex.

That history is the beginning of these cases. The respondents say it should be the end as well. To them, it would demean a timeless institution if the concept and lawful status of marriage were extended to two persons of the same sex. Marriage, in their view, is by its nature a gender-differentiated union of man and woman. This view long has been held—and continues to be held—in good faith by reasonable and sincere people here and throughout the world.

The petitioners acknowledge this history but contend that these cases cannot end there. Were their intent to demean the revered idea and reality of marriage, the petitioners' claims would be of a different order. But that is neither their purpose nor their submission. To the contrary, it is the enduring importance of marriage that underlies the petitioners' contentions. This, they say, is their whole point. Far from seeking to devalue marriage, the petitioners seek it for themselves because of their respect—and need—for its privileges and responsibilities. And their immutable nature dictates that same-sex marriage is their only real path to this profound commitment.

Recounting the circumstances of three of these cases illustrates the urgency of the petitioners' cause from their perspective. Petitioner James Obergefell, a plaintiff in the Ohio case, met John Arthur over two decades ago. They fell in love and started a life together, establishing a lasting, committed relation. In 2011, however, Arthur was diagnosed with amyotrophic lateral sclerosis, or ALS. This debilitating disease is progressive, with no known cure. Two years ago, Obergefell and Arthur decided to commit to one another, resolving to marry before Arthur died. To fulfill their mutual promise, they traveled from Ohio to Maryland, where same-sex marriage was legal. It was difficult for Arthur to move, and so the couple were wed inside a medical transport plane as it remained on the tarmac in Baltimore. Three months later, Arthur died. Ohio law does not permit Obergefell to be listed as the surviving spouse on Arthur's death certificate. By statute, they must remain strangers even in death, a state-imposed separation Obergefell deems "hurtful for the rest of time." He brought suit to be shown as the surviving spouse on Arthur's death certificate.

April DeBoer and Jayne Rowse are co-plaintiffs in the case from Michigan. They celebrated a commitment ceremony to honor their permanent relation in 2007. They both work as nurses, DeBoer in a neonatal unit and Rowse in an emergency unit. In 2009, DeBoer and Rowse fostered and then adopted a baby boy. Later that same year, they welcomed another son into their family. The new baby, born prematurely and abandoned by his biological mother, required around-the-clock care. The next year, a baby girl with special needs joined their family. Michigan, however, permits only opposite-sex married couples or single individuals to adopt, so each child can have only one woman as his or her legal parent. If an emergency were to arise, schools and hospitals may treat the three children as if they had only one parent. And, were tragedy to befall either DeBoer or Rowse, the other would have no legal rights over the children she had not been permitted to adopt. This couple seeks relief from the continuing uncertainty their unmarried status creates in their lives.

Army Reserve Sergeant First Class Ijpe DeKoe and his partner Thomas Kostura, co-plaintiffs in the Tennessee case, fell in love. In 2011, DeKoe received orders to deploy to Afghanistan. Before leaving, he and Kostura married in New York. A week later, DeKoe began his deployment, which lasted for almost a year. When he returned, the two settled in Tennessee, where DeKoe works full-time for the Army Reserve. Their lawful marriage is stripped from them whenever they reside in Tennessee, returning and disappearing as they travel across state lines. DeKoe, who served this Nation to preserve the freedom the Constitution protects, must endure a substantial burden.

The cases now before the Court involve other petitioners as well, each with their own experiences. Their stories reveal that they seek not to denigrate marriage but rather to live their lives, or honor their spouses' memory, joined by its bond. …

III

Under the Due Process Clause of the Fourteenth Amendment, no State shall "deprive any person of life, liberty, or property, without due process of law." The fundamental liberties protected by this Clause include most of the rights enumerated in the Bill of Rights. In addition these liberties extend to certain personal choices central to individual dignity and autonomy, including intimate choices that define personal identity and beliefs.

The identification and protection of fundamental rights is an enduring part of the judicial duty to interpret the Constitution. That responsibility, however, "has not been reduced to any formula." Rather, it requires courts to exercise reasoned judgment in identifying interests of the person so fundamental that the State must accord them its respect. See ibid. That process is guided by many of the same considerations relevant to analysis of other constitutional provisions that set forth broad principles rather than specific requirements. History and tradition guide and discipline this inquiry but do not set its outer boundaries. See Lawrence, supra, at 572. That method respects our history and learns from it without allowing the past alone to rule the present.

The nature of injustice is that we may not always see it in our own times. The generations that wrote and ratified the Bill of Rights and the Fourteenth Amendment did not presume to know the extent of freedom in all of its dimensions, and so they entrusted to future generations a charter protecting the right of all persons to enjoy liberty as we learn its meaning. When new insight reveals discord between the Constitution's central protections and a received legal stricture, a claim to liberty must be addressed.

Applying these established tenets, the Court has long held the right to marry is protected by the Constitution. In *Loving v. Virginia,* which invalidated bans on interracial unions, a unanimous Court held marriage is "one of the vital personal rights essential to the orderly pursuit of happiness by free men." The Court reaffirmed that holding in *Zablocki v. Redhail,* which held the right to marry was burdened by a law prohibiting fathers who were behind on child support from marrying. The Court again applied this principle in *Turner v. Safley,* which held the right to marry was abridged by regulations limiting the privilege of prison inmates to marry. Over time and in other contexts, the Court has reiterated that the right to marry is fundamental under the Due Process Clause. ...

There is no difference between same- and opposite-sex couples with respect to this principle. Yet by virtue of their exclusion from that institution, same-sex couples are denied the constellation of benefits that the States have linked to marriage. This harm results in more than just material burdens. Same-sex couples are consigned to an instability many opposite-sex couples would deem intolerable in their own lives. As the State itself makes marriage all the more precious by the significance it attaches to it, exclusion from that status has the effect of teaching that gays and lesbians are unequal in important respects. It demeans gays and lesbians for the State to lock them out of a central institution of the Nation's society. Same-sex couples, too, may aspire to the transcendent purposes of marriage and seek fulfillment in its highest meaning.

The limitation of marriage to opposite-sex couples may long have seemed natural and just, but its inconsistency with the central meaning of the fundamental right to marry is now manifest. With that knowledge must come the recognition that laws excluding same-sex couples from the marriage right impose stigma and injury of the kind prohibited by our basic charter. ...

The right of same-sex couples to marry that is part of the liberty promised by the Fourteenth Amendment is derived, too, from that Amendment's guarantee of the equal protection of the laws. The Due Process Clause and the Equal Protection Clause are connected in a profound way, though they set forth independent principles. Rights implicit in liberty and rights secured by equal protection may rest on different precepts and are not always co-extensive, yet in some instances each may be instructive as to the meaning and reach of the other. In any particular case one Clause may be thought to capture the essence of the right in a more accurate and comprehensive way, even as the two Clauses may converge in the identification and definition of the right. ...

IV

... This is not the first time the Court has been asked to adopt a cautious approach to recognizing and protecting fundamental rights. In Bowers, a bare majority upheld a law criminalizing same-sex intimacy. That approach might have been viewed as a cautious endorsement of the democratic process, which had only just begun to consider the rights of gays and lesbians. Yet, in effect, Bowers upheld state action that denied gays and lesbians a fundamental right and caused them pain and humiliation. As evidenced by the dissents in that case, the facts and principles necessary to a correct holding were known to the Bowers Court. That is why Lawrence held Bowers was "not correct when it was decided." Although Bowers was eventually repudiated in Lawrence, men and women were harmed in the interim, and the substantial effects of these injuries no doubt lingered long after Bowers was overruled. Dignitary wounds cannot always be healed with the stroke of a pen. ...

No union is more profound than marriage, for it embodies the highest ideals of love, fidelity, devotion, sacrifice, and family. In forming a marital union, two people become something greater than once they were. As some of the petitioners in these cases demonstrate, marriage embodies a love that may endure even past death. It would misunderstand these men and women to say they disrespect the idea of marriage. Their plea is that they do respect it, respect it so deeply that they seek to find its fulfillment for themselves. Their hope is not to be condemned to live in loneliness, excluded from one of civilization's oldest institutions. They ask for equal dignity in the eyes of the law. The Constitution grants them that right.

The judgment of the Court of Appeals for the Sixth Circuit is reversed.

It is so ordered.

Chronology

1868 The Fourteenth Amendment is ratified.

1917 The Immigration Act of 1917 bans gay and lesbian people from immigrating to the US.

1972 The US Supreme Court declines to hear *Baker v. Nelson*.

1973 Maryland becomes the first state to ban same-sex marriage.

1989 The New York State Court of Appeals rules that a gay couple living together for more than ten years qualified as a family.

1990 The immigration ban on gay and lesbian people is lifted.

1996 The Supreme Court of Hawaii rules that the state has to present compelling evidence that it is necessary to deny marriage licenses to same-sex couples.

The Defense of Marriage Act (DOMA) passes in Congress and becomes law

1998 Hawaii voters give the state the power to ban same-sex marriages.

2000 Vermont becomes the first state to offer civil unions.

2003 The *Lawrence v. Texas* ruling strikes down state bans on sexual activity between two people of the same gender.

2004 Massachusetts becomes the first state to legalize same-sex marriage

2005 Canada legalizes same-sex marriages.

November 9, 2010 Windsor files against the federal government challenging the constitutionality of DOMA.

2013 The Supreme Court ruling in *United States v. Windsor* strikes down part of DOMA.

July 11, 2013 Obergefell and Arthur are married in Maryland.

July 19, 2013 Attorney Al Gerhardstein sues the state of Ohio on behalf of Obergefell and Arthur.

December 23, 2013 Judge Black rules that Ohio must recognize same-sex marriages performed in other states on death certificates.

January 24, 2014 The state of Ohio appeals Black's ruling.

April 25, 2014 The Sixth Circuit Court of Appeals decides to hear the same-sex marriage cases.

November 6, 2014 The Sixth Circuit Court of Appeals overturns district court rulings permitting same-sex marriage in Kentucky, Michigan, Ohio, and Tennessee.

April 28, 2015 Oral Arguments are held in *Obergefell v. Hodges.*

June 26, 2015 The Supreme Court rules in *Obergefell v. Hodges,* affirming that same-sex couples have the right to marry.

Chapter Notes

Chapter 1. Unequal in Ohio

1. Adam Liptak, "Justices Extend Benefits To Gay Couples; Allow Same-Sex Marriages In California," *New York Times*, June 27, 2013.

2. Bill Chappell, "Supreme Court Declares Same-Sex Marriage Legal in All 50 States," *NPR*, June 26, 2015, http://www.npr.org/sections/thetwo-way/2015/06/26/417717613/supreme-court-rules-all-states-must-allow-same-sex-marriages.

3. Clarence Haynes, "Jim Obergefell," Biography.com, http://www.biography.com/people/jim-obergefell.

4. Julie Zimmerman, "Ohio Man Who Challenged Same-Sex Marriage Ban Has Died," *USA Today*, October 22, 2013, http://www.usatoday.com/story/news/nation/2013/10/22/john-arthur-obit-same-sex-marriage-ban-challenge/3150525/.

5. Lina Guillen, "Marriage Rights and Benefits," *Nolo*, May 11, 2016, http://www.nolo.com/legal-encyclopedia/marriage-rights-benefits-30190.html.

6. Kevin Rector, "A Unique Maryland Marriage Sits at Center of Supreme Court Case Considering Gay Nuptials," *Baltimore Sun*, March 13, 2015, http://www.baltimoresun.com/features/gay-in-maryland/gay-matters/bs-gm-obergefell-scotus-connection-20150313-story.html.

7. Erik Ortiz, "Supreme Court Gay Marriage Debate Puts Ohio Man Jim Obergefell in Center," *NBC News*, April 26, 2015, http://www.nbcnews.com/politics/supreme-court/supreme-courts-gay-marriage-debate-puts-ohio-man-jim-obergefell-n347836.

8. Liptak, "Justices Extend Benefits."

9. Michael S. Rosenwald, "How Jim Obergefell Became the Face of the Supreme Court Gay Marriage Case," *Washington Post*, April 6, 2015, https://www.washingtonpost.com/local/how-jim-obergefell-became-the-face-of-the-supreme-court-gay-marriage-case/2015/04/06/3740433c-d958-11e4-b3f2-607bd612aeac_story.html.

10. Chris Geidner, "Two Years After His Husband's Death, Jim Obergefell is Still Fighting for the Right to be Married," *BuzzFeed*, March 22, 2015, https://www.buzzfeed.com/chrisgeidner/his-huband-died-in-2013-but-jim-obergefell-is-still-fighting?utm_term=.qmVG4XKgP#.mbZy9RDmW.

11. *Obergefell et al. v. Kasich et al.* (United States District Court Southern District of Ohio Western Division, Verified Complaint for Temporary Restraining Order and Declarative and Injunctive Relief), http://www.clearinghouse.net/chDocs/public/PB-OH-0003-0002.pdf.

12. *Obergefell et al. v. Kasich et al.* (Temporary Restraining Order, July 22, 2013), https://docs.justia.com/cases/federal/district-courts/ohio/ohsdce/1:2013cv00501/164617/14.

13. Juliet Eilperin, "Federal Judge Recognizes Gay Married Couple in Ohio, Despite State Ban," *Washington Post*, July 23, 2013, https://www.washingtonpost.com/news/post-politics/wp/2013/07/23/federal-judge-recognizes-out-of-state-gay-married-couple-in-oh-despite-state-ban-in-temporary-order/.

Chapter 2. Marriage in the United States

1. "Timeline of LGBT History in Virginia and the United States," Virginia Department of Human Resources, 2015, http://www.dhr.virginia.gov/NewDominion/index.htm.

2. Ibid.

3. "Matter of LaRochelle in Deportation Hearings," US Department of Justice, December 4, 1965, https://www.justice.gov/sites/default/files/eoir/legacy/2012/08/27/1538.pdf.

4. Immigration and Nationality Act Amendments of 1965 Pub. L. No. 89-236, 79 Stat. 911. (1965), http://library.uwb.edu/static/usimmigration/79%20stat%20911.pdf.

5. "*Lawrence v. Texas,*" Chicago-Kent College of Law at Illinois Tech, Oyez, https://www.oyez.org/cases/2002/02-102.

6. Lyle Denniston, "Gay Marriage and Baker v. Nelson," *SCOTUSblog*, July 4, 2012, http://www.scotusblog.com/2012/07/gay-marriage-and-baker-v-nelson/.

7. "Baker v. Nelson," Bloomburg Law, October 15, 1971, http://www2.bloomberglaw.com/public/desktop/document/Baker_v_Nelson_291_Minn_310_191_NW2d_185_1971_Court_Opinion?1464128632.

8. Barbara Bradley Hagerty, "Maryland Judge Rejects Gay-Marriage Ban," *NPR*, January 20, 2006, http://www.npr.org/templates/story/story.php?storyId=5164355.

9. Judith Scherr, "Berkeley, Activists Set Milestone for Domestic Partnerships in 1984," *San Jose Mercury News*, June 28, 2013, http://www.mercurynews.com/alameda-county/ci_23561502/berkeley-activists-set-milestone-domestic-partnerships-1984.

10. Karen M. Dunak, "The Secret History of Gay Marriage," *Salon*, September 8, 2013, http://www.salon.com/2013/09/08/the_secret_history_of_gay_marriage/.

11. Philip S. Gutis, "Small Steps Toward Acceptance Renew Debate on Gay Marriage," *New York Times*, November 5, 1989, http://www.nytimes.com/1989/11/05/weekinreview/ideas-trends-small-steps-toward-acceptance-renew-debate-on-gay-marriage.html.

12. Ibid.

13. *Baehr et al. v. Miike, et al.* (First Circuit Court, State of Hawaii, Findings of Facts and Conclusions of Law, December 3, 1996), http://www.lambdalegal.org/in-court/legal-docs/baehr_hi_19961203_decision-hi-circuit-court.

14. Ibid.

15. Ibid.

16. Carey Goldberg, "Hawaii Judge Ends Gay-Marriage Ban," *New York Times*, December 4, 1996, http://www.nytimes.com/1996/12/04/us/hawaii-judge-ends-gay-marriage-ban.html.

17. Mark Niesse, "Hawaii is Latest Civil Unions Battleground," *Associated Press*, March 3, 2009, http://www.webcitation.org/5ewPtDMg0.

18. Nick Ramsey, "How—and Why—DOMA Became Law in 1996," *MSNBC*, March 30, 2013, http://www.msnbc.com/the-last-word/how-and-why-doma-became-law-1996.

19. Niesse, "Hawaii is Latest Civil Unions Battleground."

20. Ibid.

21. Ramsey, "How—and Why—DOMA Became Law in 1996."

22. *The Defense of Marriage Act*, Library of Congress, 1996, http://thomas.loc.gov/cgi-bin/bdquery/z?d104:h.r.03396:.

23. Ibid.

24. Ramsey, "How—and Why—DOMA Became Law in 1996."

25. Defense of Marriage Act (Final Vote Results for Roll Call 316 on Passage, July 12, 1996), http://clerk.house.gov/evs/1996/roll316.xml.

26. Defense of Marriage Act (On Passage of the Bill [h.r.3396]: Vote Summary), http://www.senate.gov/legislative/LIS/roll_call_lists/roll_call_vote_cfm.cfm?congress=104&session=2&vote=00280.

27. Bob Barr, "No Defending the Defense of Marriage Act," *Los Angeles Times*, January 5, 2009, http://www.latimes.com/la-oe-barr5-2009jan05-story.html.

28. Peter Baker, "Now in Defense of Gay Marriage, Bill Clinton," *New York Times*, March 25, 2013, http://www.nytimes.com/2013/03/26/us/politics/bill-clintons-decision-and-regret-on-defense-of-marriage-act.html?_r=0.

29. "Same-Sex Marriage, State by State," Pew Research Center, June 26, 2015, http://www.pewforum.org/2015/06/26/same-sex-marriage-state-by-state/.

30. Susan Kreifels, "A Quiet Revolution," *Honolulu Star-Bulletin*, May 8, 1998, http://archives.starbulletin.com/98/05/08/news/story2.html.

31. "Timeline of LGBT History in Virginia and the United States," Virginia Department of Human Resources.

32. Kailani Koenig, "Ten Years Ago, Massachusetts Introduced Us to Gay Marriage," *MSNBC*, May 16, 2014, http://www.msnbc.com/msnbc/ten-years-ago-massachusetts-introduced-us-gay-marriage.

33. Ibid.

34. Ibid.

35. Kathleen Burge, "SJC: Gay Marriage Legal in Massachusetts," *Boston Globe*, November 18, 2013, http://archive.boston.com/news/local/massachusetts/articles/2003/11/18/sjc_gay_marriage_legal_in_mass/.

36. Ibid.

37. Frank Phillips and Rick Klein, "50% in Poll Back SJC Ruling on Gay Marriage," *Boston Globe*, November 23, 2003, http://archive.boston.com/news/local/articles/2003/11/23/50_in_poll_back_sjc_ruling_on_gay_marriage/.

38. Koenig, "Ten Years Ago."

39. Drew DeSilver, "How Many Same-Sex Marriages in the U.S.? At Least 71,165, Probably More," Pew Research Center, June 26, 2013, http://www.pewresearch.org/fact-tank/2013/06/26/how-many-same-sex-marriages-in-the-u-s-at-least-71165-probably-more/.

40. Pete Williams and Erin McClam, "Supreme Court Strikes Down Defense of Marriage Act, Paves Way for Gay Marriage to Resume in California," *NBC News*, June 26, 2013, http://nbcpolitics.nbcnews.com/_news/2013/06/26/19151971-supreme-court-strikes-down-defense-of-marriage-act-paves-way-for-gay-marriage-to-resume-in-california.

41. Robin Tyler, "How Roberta Kaplan Met Edie Windsor and Changed History," *The Advocate*, October 19, 2015, http://www.advocate.com/commentary/2015/10/19/how-roberta-kaplan-met-edie-windsor-and-changed-history.

42. Ibid.

43. Williams and McClam, "Supreme Court Strikes Down Defense of Marriage Act."

Chapter 3. A Growing Case

1. "Justice 101: Introduction to the Federal Court System," United States Department of Justice, https://www.justice.gov/usao/justice-101/federal-courts.

2. Ibid.

3. Ibid.

4. Ibid.

5. Ibid.

6. "Judges Biographical Sketch," United States District Court Southern District of Ohio, http://www.ohsd.uscourts.gov/judges-biographical-sketch.

7. Julie Zimmerman, "Ohio Man Who Challenged Same-Sex Marriage Ban has Died," *USA Today*, October 22, 2013, http://www.usatoday.com/story/news/nation/2013/10/22/john-arthur-obit-same-sex-marriage-ban-challenge/3150525/.

8. Associated Press, "Federal Judge Sides With Ohio Gay Couple on Death Certificate," *Los Angeles Times*, September 4, 2013, http://www.latimes.com/nation/nationnow/la-na-nn-ohio-same-sex-marriage-20130904-story.html.

9. *Obergefell et al. v. Wymyslo et al.* (Order Denying the Motion to Dismiss of Defendant Dr. Theodore Wymyslo, November 1, 2013), http://www.clearinghouse.net/chDocs/public/PB-OH-0003-0004.pdf.

10. *Obergefell et al. v. Wymyslo et al.* (Amended Complaint, September 26, 2016), https://docs.justia.com/cases/federal/district-courts/ohio/ohsdce/1:2013cv00501/164617/33.

11. Ibid.

12. Ibid.

13. Vincent Bzdek, "Ohio's Ban on Gay Marriage Ruled Unconstitutional in Limited Case," *Washington Post*, December 23, 2013, https://www.washingtonpost.com/blogs/govbeat/wp/2013/12/23/ohios-ban-on-gay-marriage-ruled-unconstitutional-in-limited-case/.

14. *Obergefell et al. v. Wymyslo et al.* (US District Court Southern District of Ohio Western Division, Final Order Granting Plaintiffs' Motion for Declaratory Judgment and Permanent Injunction, December 23, 2013), https://cases.justia.com/federal/districtcourts/ohio/ohsdce/1:2013cv00501/164617/65/0.pdf?ts=1387840357.

15. US Constitution Amendment XIV, Section 2–5, http://www.senate.gov/civics/constitution_item/constitution.htm.

16. Ibid.

17. *Obergefell et al. v. Wymyslo et al.* (US District Court Southern District of Ohio Western Division, Final Order Granting Plaintiffs' Motion for Declaratory Judgment and Permanent Injunction, December 23, 2013), https://cases.justia.com/federal/district-courts/ohio/ohsdce/1:2013cv00501/164617/65/0.pdf?ts=1387840357.

18. Ibid.

19. Ibid.

20. "Obergefell v. Hodges," American Civil Liberties Union of Ohio, http://www.acluohio.org/archives/cases/obergefell-v-hodges.

21. *Henry et al. v. Hodges* (Supreme Court of the United States, Joint Petition for a Writ of Certiorari)., https://www.aclu.org/sites/default/files/assets/henry_v__hodges__obergefell_v__hodges_joint_petition_for_a_writ_of_certiorari.pdf.

22. Ibid.

23. Ibid.

24. *DeBoer et al. v. Snyder et al.* (United States District Court Eastern District of Michigan Southern Division, Findings of Fact and Conclusions of Law, March 21, 2014), https://cases.justia.com/federal/district-courts/michigan/miedce/2:2012cv10285/266068/151/0.pdf?ts=1395489164.

25. Ibid.

26. Rebecca Cook, "Ruling to Strike Down Michigan Gay Marriage Ban Put on Hold," *Reuters*, March 22, 2014, http://www.reuters.com/article/us-usa-gaymarriage-michigan-idUSBREA2K1Y420140322.

27. *Bourke et al. v. Beshear et al.* (United States District Court Western District of Kentucky, Memorandum Opinion), https://www.scribd.com/doc/206724639/GREGORY-BOURKE-et-al-V-STEVE-BESHEAR-et-al.

28. *Love et al. v. Beshear et al.* (United States District Court Western District of Kentucky at Louisville, Memorandum Opinion), http://www.clearinghouse.net/chDocs/public/PB-KY-0001-0006.pdf.

29. Ibid.

30. *Tanco et al. v. Haslam et al.* (United States District Court for the Middle District of Tennessee Nashville Division, Memorandum), https://www.scribd.com/doc/212514998/TANCO-v-HASLAM.

Chapter 4. A Setback in Court

1. Emily Wood, "Gay marriage cases heard in Cincinnati draw crowds on both sides," *WLWT*, August 6, 2014, http://www.wlwt.com/news/gay-marriage-cases-heard-in-cincinnati-draw-crowds-on-both-sides/27333352.

2. "About Federal Courts: Appeals," Administrative Offices of the United States Courts, http://www.uscourts.gov/about-federal-courts/types-cases/appeals.

3. "Deborah Louise Cook," The Supreme Court of Ohio and the Ohio Judicial System, https://www.supremecourt.ohio.gov/SCO/formerjustices/bios/cook.asp.

4. Ariane De Vogue, "How a Cincinnati Judge Could Shape the Gay Marriage Case," CNN, April 24, 2015, http://www.cnn.com/2015/04/24/politics/jeffrey-sutton-gay-marriage/.

5. Jessica Bliss, "Tennessee Judge's Epic Firsts are Historic, Unparallelled," *Tennessean*, March 26, 2015, http://www.tennessean.com/story/news/2015/03/26/tennessee-judge-epic-firsts/70462294/.

6. Wood, "Gay Marriage Cases Heard in Cincinnati."

7. "Michigan Same-Sex Marriage Oral Arguments," C-SPAN, August 6, 2014, http://www.c-span.org/video/?320907-1/michigan-samesex-marriage-oral-argument-audio.

8. Ibid.

9. Ibid.

10. "Ohio Same-Sex Marriage Oral Arguments," C-SPAN, August 6, 2014, http://www.c-span.org/video/?320907-2/ohio-samesex-marriage-oral-argument-audio.

11. Ibid.

12. *Bourke et al. & Love et al. v. Beshear et al.* (Brief for Respondent), https://www.aclu.org/sites/default/files/field_document/brief_for_respondent_ky.pdf.

13. *Bourke et al. & Love et al. v. Beshear et al.,* http://player.piksel.com/p/w70z36r9.

14. *Tanco et al. v. Haslam et al.,* http://player.piksel.com/p/w70z36r9.

15. Ibid.

16. *DeBoer et al. v. Snyder et al.* (United States Court of Appeals for the Sixth Circuit, Opinion. November 6, 2014), http://www.ca6.uscourts.gov/opinions.pdf/14a0275p-06.pdf.

17. Ibid.

18. Ibid.

19. Ibid.

20. Ibid.

21. Ibid.

22. Dale Carpenter, "Justice Ginsburg: 'no urgency' yet on same-sex marriage," *Washington Post*, September 16, 2014, https://www.washingtonpost.com/news/volokh-conspiracy/wp/2014/09/16/justice-ginsburg-no-urgency-yet-on-same-sex-marriage/.

Chapter 5. A Case for the Plaintiff

1. Amisha Padnani and Celina Fang, "Same-Sex Marriage: Landmark Decisions and Precedents," *New York Times*, June 26, 2015, http://www.nytimes.com/interactive/2015/06/26/us/samesex-marriage-landmarks.html?_r=0.

2. "Changing Attitudes on Gay Marriage," Pew Research Center, May 12, 2016, http://www.pewforum.org/2016/05/12/changing-attitudes-on-gay-marriage/.

3. "Obergefell v. Hodges," Chicago-Kent College of Law at Illinois Tech, Oyez, https://www.oyez.org/cases/2014/14-556.

4. "Party Briefs on the Merits," Supreme Court of the United States, http://www.supremecourt.gov/ObergefellHodges/PartyBriefs/.

5. Ruthann Robson, "Guide to the Amicus Briefs in Obergefell V. Hodges: The Same-Sex Marriage Cases," *Constitutional Law Prof Blog*, April 16, 2015, http://lawprofessors.typepad.com/conlaw/2015/04/guide-to-amicus-briefs-in-obergefell-v-hodges-the-same-sex-marriage-cases.html.

6. Ibid.

7. Ariane De Vogue, "Meet the Lawyers Who Will Argue the Gay Marriage Case," CNN, April 27, 2015, http://www.cnn.com/2015/04/24/politics/supreme-court-gay-marriage-lawyers/.

8. "MacArthur Fellows Program: Meet the Class of 2017--Mary L. Bonauto," MacArthur Foundation, September 17, 2014, https://www.macfound.org/fellows/909/.

9. De Vogue, "Meet the Lawyers."

10. Ibid.

11. *The Constitution of the United States*, Amendment 5.

12. *Meyer v. State of Nebraska*, 262 U.S. 390 (1923).

13. David A. Fahrenthold, "Outside Supreme Court, Gay-Marriage Supporters Jubilant and Expectant," *Washington Post*, April 28, 2015, https://www.washingtonpost.com/politics/excited-crowds-gather-at-supreme-court-as-gay-marriage-case-is-heard/2015/04/28/b8e6e6fa-eda0-11e4-8666-a1d756d0218e_story.html?hpid=z1.

14. Fred Barbash, Mark Berman, and Sandhya Somashekhar, "Supreme Court Hears Same-Sex Marriage Case: Who Said What (With Audio)," *Washington Post*, April 28, 2015, https://www.washingtonpost.com/news/post-nation/wp/2015/04/28/supreme-court-hears-arguments-in-same-sex-marriage-case-obergefell-v-hodges-today/.

15. Ibid.

16. Ibid.

17. Ibid.

18. Ibid.

19. Ibid.

20. Ibid.

21. Ibid.

22. Ibid.

23. Ibid.

24. Ibid.

Chapter 6. The Defense Argues

1. *DeBoer et al. v. Snyder et al.* (Appeal From the US District Court, Eastern District of Michigan), http://www.clearinghouse.net/chDocs/public/PB-MI-0004-0036.pdf.

2. *Obergefell et al. v. Hodges et al.* (Brief for the Respondent), https://www.aclu.org/sites/default/files/field_document/brief_for_respondent_oh_dept_of_health.pdf.

3. Lyle Denniston, "Preview on Same-Sex Marriage--Part II, the States' Views," *SCOTUSblog*, April 14, 2015, http://www.scotusblog.com/2015/04/preview-on-same-sex-marriage-part-ii-the-states-views/.

4. Ibid.

5. Ariane De Vogue, "Meet the Lawyers Who Will Argue the Gay Marriage Case," CNN, April 27, 2015, http://www.cnn.com/2015/04/24/politics/supreme-court-gay-marriage-lawyers/.

6. *Obergefell et al. v. Hodges et al.* (Supreme Court of the United States Oral Arguments, Question 1), http://www.supremecourt.gov/oral_arguments/argument_transcripts/14-556q1_11o2.pdf.

7. Ibid.

8. Ibid.

9. Ibid.

10. Ibid.

11. De Vogue, "Meet the Lawyers."

12. *Obergefell et al. v. Hodges et al.* (Supreme Court of the United States Oral Arguments, Question 2), http://www.supremecourt.gov/oral_arguments/argument_transcripts/14-556q2_f2ah.pdf.

13. Dan Roberts and Sabrina Siddiqui, "Anthony Kennedy: How One Man's Evolution Legalized Marriage for Millions," *Guardian*, June 26, 2015, http://www.theguardian.com/us-news/2015/jun/26/kennedy-ruling-gay-marriage-supreme-court.

Chapter 7. The Justices Decide

1. Robert Barnes, "Supreme Court Rules Gay Couples Nationwide Have a Right to Marry," *Washington Post*, June 26, 2015, https://www.washingtonpost.com/politics/gay-marriage-and-other-major-rulings-at-the-supreme-court/2015/06/25/ef75a120-1b6d-11e5-bd7f-4611a60dd8e5_story.html.

2. Ibid.

3. Ibid.

4. Ibid.

5. *Obergefell et al. v. Hodges et al.* (Syllabus), http://www.supremecourt.gov/opinions/14pdf/14-556_3204.pdf.

6. Ibid.

7. Ibid.

8. Ibid.

9. Ibid.

10. Ibid.

11. "Mildred Loving, 40 Years Later," *Atlantic*, June 18, 2007, http://www.theatlantic.com/daily-dish/archive/2007/06/mildred-loving-40-years-later/227582/.

12. Barnes, "Supreme Court Rules."

13. *Obergefell et al. v. Hodges et al.* (Syllabus), http://www.supremecourt.gov/opinions/14pdf/14-556_3204.pdf.

14. Ibid.

15. Ibid.

16. Ibid.

17. Ibid.

18. Ibid.

19. Ibid.

20. Ibid.

21. "Supreme Court Rules on Same-Sex Marriage: Joy, Defiance and Questions Result," *Los Angeles Times*, June 26, 2015, http://www.latimes.com/nation/la-na-gay-marriage-ruling-supreme-court-live-htmlstory.html.

22. Barnes, "Supreme Court Rules."

23. Ibid.

Glossary

activist One who campaigns for a cause with the goal of achieving political or social change.

amendment A change of or addition to a document such as a bill or constitution.

appeal To apply for the transfer of a case to a higher court for a new hearing.

benefits Advantages such as rights and privileges granted through a contract.

bill A draft of a proposed law that has not been passed or enacted.

brief A document filed in court making an argument for one side of a case.

civil union A legally recognized relationship, usually between a same-sex couple, that grants many of the rights of marriage.

consolidate To Combine two or more legal actions into a single action through court order.

death certificate An official document signed by a doctor stating the date, fact, and cause of a person's death.

defendant The party against whom a claim or charge is brought in a court.

discrimination Prejudicial treatment of members of a certain group, such as class, religion, race, gender, or sexual orientation.

landmark case A court case, usually heard before the Supreme Court, that establishes significant new legal principles or standards.

marriage license A legal document issued by a government authority that allows a couple to marry.

nominate To officially propose someone as a candidate for a position or office.

opinion In law, a judge's written explanation of the reasoning and legal principles used in deciding a case.

petitioner The party who files a petition in court, especially if appealing after losing in a lower court.

plaintiff The party who initiates a legal action by filing a complaint in court.

precedent A judicial decision that may be used as a standard in deciding future similar cases.

privilege An advantage, immunity, or exception granted to an individual or group.

procreation Reproduction, or the production of children.

respondent During a court appeal, the party against whom the appeal is filed.

restraining order A court order prohibiting a person from doing a particular act.

unconstitutional In violation of one or more provisions of the US Constitution or other constitution.

valid Possessing legal effect or force.

Further Reading

Books

Becker, Jo. *Forcing the Spring: Inside the Fight for Marriage Equality*. New York, NY: Penguin Press, 2014.

Faderman, Lillian. *The Gay Revolution: The Story of the Struggle*. New York, NY: Simon & Schuster, 2015.

Frank, Walter. *Law and the Gay Rights Story: The Long Search for Equal Justice in a Divided Democracy*. New Brunswick, NJ: Rutgers University Press, 2014.

Kaplan, Roberta. *Then Comes Marriage: United States V. Windsor and the Defeat of DOMA*. New York, NY: W. W. Norton & Company, 2015.

Pierceson, Jason. *Same-Sex Marriage in the United States: The Road to the Supreme Court*. Lanham, MD: Rowman & Littlefield Publishers, 2013.

Websites

American Civil Liberties Union (ACLU)

www.aclu.org

The American Civil Liberties Union works in the courts, legislatures and communities to defend and preserve the individual rights and liberties guaranteed by the Constitution and laws of the United States.

The Federalist Society for Law and Public Policy Studies

www.fed-soc.org

The Federalist Society for Law and Public Policy Studies is a group of conservatives and libertarians interested in the current state of the legal order. It is founded on the principles that the state exists to preserve freedom, that the separation of governmental powers is central to our Constitution, and that it is emphatically the province and duty of the judiciary to say what the law is, not what it should be.

GLBTQ Legal Advocates & Defenders (GLAD)

www.glad.org

Through strategic litigation, public policy advocacy, and education, GLBTQ Legal Advocates & Defenders works in New England and nationally to create a just society free of discrimination based on gender identity and expression, HIV status, and sexual orientation.

Index

P

Powell, Lewis, 43
Proposition 8, 11, 12

R

Reagan, Ronald, 31, 56, 76
Roberts, John, 56, 64, 65, 67, 73,
74, 76, 86, 87
Roberts, Paulette, 11
Rogers, Brittni, 37
Romney, Mitt, 26
Rowse, Jane, 38

S

Scalia, Antonin, 43, 56, 67, 76,
86, 87
*Schuette v. Coalition to Defend
Affirmative Action*, 71
Sotomayor, Sonia, 56, 73, 76, 81
Spyer, Thea, 26
Stanyar, Carole, 45
State Bar of California, 19
Sutton, Jeffrey S., 42, 43

T

Tanco, Valeria, 40
Tanco v. Haslam, 40, 41, 43,
52, 58
Tennessee, 31, 32, 40, 42, 43, 45,
48, 57, 58, 60, 74, 75
Texas, 91

Thomas, Clarence, 56, 64, 76,
86, 89
Trauger, Aleta A., 32, 40

U

United States v. Windsor, 5, 6, 9,
11, 12, 13, 26, 28, 29, 36, 39,
47, 49, 53, 59, 60, 61, 62, 64,
78, 81
University of Cincinnati, 7

V

VanAntwerp, Monge, Jones,
Edwards & McCann, 46
Vermont, 25, 60
Verrilli, Donald B., 59, 60, 61,
62, 66, 72, 78

W

Washington, DC, 5, 12, 19, 26,
53, 80, 81, 84, 86
Washington v. Glucksberg, 89
Whalen, Joseph, 48, 74, 75
Windsor, see *United States v.
Windsor*
Windsor, Edith, 26, 27, 28
Wriggins, Jennifer, 60
Wymyslo, Theodore, 33,
36, 43

Y

Ysunza, Lawrence, 39